WHEN HELPING STARTS TO HURT

WHEN HELPING STARTS TO HURT

A New Look at Burnout Among Psychotherapists

William N. Grosch, M.D., M. Div.
Director, Psychiatric Outpatient Clinic, Albany Medical College
Director, Pastoral Services, Capital District Psychiatric Center, Albany, New York

David C. Olsen, Ph.D., C.S.W.
Executive Director, The Samaritan Counseling Center of the Capital Region, Schenectady, New York

W. W. Norton & Company, Inc. • New York • London

Printed in the United States of America

First Edition

Composition by Bytheway Typesetting Services, Inc.
Manufacturing by Haddon Craftsmen, Inc.

Library of Congress Cataloging-in-Publication Data

Grosch, William N.
When helping starts to hurt : a new look at burnout among psychotherapists / William N. Grosch, David C. Olsen.
p. cm.
"A Norton professional book" –
Includes bibliographical references.
ISBN 0-393-70167-0
1. Psychotherapists–Job stress. 2. Burn out (Psychology)—Prevention. 3. Burn out (Psychology)–Treatment. 4. Psychotherapists–Mental health. I. Olsen, David C., 1952- II. Title
RC451.4.P79G76 1994
616.89'14'019–dc20 94-378 CIP

W. W. Norton & Company, Inc., 500 Fifth Avenue, New York, NY 10110
W. W. Norton & Company, Ltd., 10 Coptic Street, London WC1A 1PU

1 2 3 4 5 6 7 8 9 0

This book is dedicated to our parents:

William A. and Vivian H. Grosch

and

Wesley A. and Elaine M. Olsen

CONTENTS

ACKNOWLEDGMENTS

We are indebted to a number of people for their help in the writing of this book. In particular, we appreciate the help of Carol Calacone for her typing and Mary Barlow and Debbie Valiquette for their endless wordprocessing and correcting.

We are extremely grateful to Mike Nichols for his constant encouragement and countless hours of help and suggestions.

We are grateful to Susan Munro for her guidance, editing, and patience during the writing process.

Finally, we are thankful beyond words to our wives and children who helped us to not burn out while writing about it.

INTRODUCTION

Most of us entered the helping professions with high ideals and generous hearts. Armed with our own particular brand of salvation, we were going to change the world, or at least some of the people in it. We didn't become therapists or counselors to make money, but to help people. We started out with enormous optimism and what we thought was sufficient training and expertise. We firmly believed that this training, along with compassion and caring, would enable us to transform the lives of people who were hurting. Sadly, for many of us, idealism, optimism, and commitment gave way to disillusion and disappointment. The reality that, contrary to expectation, many of our well-intentioned efforts were ineffective and unappreciated came as a bitter irony and left us terribly disappointed. Now many of us who started out hoping to make a difference in the world have ended up hoping simply to make it to the end of the day.

This perhaps inevitable disillusionment manifests itself in a variety of ways, ranging from a sense of personal deadness, dragging through the days, watching the clock, dreading seeing another client, to a complete breakdown and an inability to go on. It may result in depression or a loss of meaning, since what we do seems to make so little difference so much of the time. At other times disillusion may manifest itself physically with chronic exhaustion, headaches, back pain, or stomach problems. The term burnout, which familiarity has robbed of impact, doesn't do justice to this tragic loss of human potential. It doesn't come close to describing the breaking of the spirit so frequently encountered in mental health professionals.

It has been said that the average therapist has a productive professional life span of ten years. Ten years before the burden of taking other people's troubles on one's shoulders erodes self-confidence and the desire to go on. Perhaps the equation should be adjusted according to setting, with agency workers, charged with reversing the ravages of poverty with kind words and food stamps, burning out faster, while those helpers lucky enough to work with more advantaged and flexible clients lasting a little longer. Sooner or later though, disillusion seems inevitable.

Too often, when professional helpers begin to hurt, they receive advice that, however well-intentioned, is banal and simplistic. Such counsel focuses on improving time management (for instance, changing the 50-minute hour to 45 minutes), planning more recreation (taking a day off here and there to play golf), rest and relaxation (getting away for a long weekend or trying some form of meditation), and more "quality time" with the family. In fact, these helpers receive the same advice they have given more frequently than they care to admit. While following these suggestions may bring a brief respite from the feelings commonly labeled burnout, in the end it is not effective.

We all know we should relax more and spend more time with our families and friends. But knowing something isn't the same as doing it. So we make an attempt to get home early for dinner, meet friends for lunch, and spend more time with the kids, but when the pressures of work reassert themselves these efforts begin to go the way of all good intentions. In the end we feel even more guilt for not relaxing more or for not putting what we know into practice. Practical advice rarely seems to change the style of our lives because its simplistic nature rarely does justice to the complexity of our problems. Burnout is no exception.

How, then, are we to understand the stubborn persistence of burnout? While most people would agree that burnout is a multifaceted problem in the helping professions, and while there is an abundance of workshops and seminars on the topic, most of the responses to the problem offer little more than band aid solutions. When attempts are made to understand more thoroughly the underpinnings of burnout, several basic themes emerge. Some writers, for example, see at least part of the problem as located in the psyche of the helping professional. They discuss the difficulties of the "type-A" personality, or the excessive idealism of some in the profession, or even the low self-esteem of many professionals that causes them to take on more and more work in an ill-fated attempt to bolster their personal sense of adequacy. Other writers locate the problem of burnout in the human service systems. They suggest that many aspects of these work systems are more than capable of producing emotional depletion. They cite, for example, funding cutbacks that force longer hours with less clinical support, mountains of paperwork and red tape, caseloads that are too high, and multiproblem clients burdened by poverty and despair, with few resources of their own and easily able to drain those of their helpers. Still others emphasize problems in either the professional's present family or his/her family of origin that predispose the helper to professional exhaustion. For example, dealing with death, birth, remarriage, or adoption, serious illness of a family member, a spouse who never seems to understand the long hours and emotional toll demanded by the profession, or having one's own child getting in trouble in school all threaten one's sense of competence, not to mention making it progressively more difficult to be therapeutically present for clients.

Obviously, advice on how to deal with burnout will be influenced by one's point of view as to what caused the problem in the first place. Unfortunately, much of the advice seems fragmented, pointing to theoretical frames of reference that are incomplete and underdeveloped in the literature. We believe that in order to deal adequately with the problem of professional exhaustion, an integrated theory must be constructed which encompasses the various underlying causes. Only after such an integrated paradigm is developed can valid and effective solutions for prevention and treatment of burnout be formulated.

As a first step in paradigm construction, we will survey the literature on burnout, isolating themes that appear frequently in discussions of occupational exhaustion. This is not intended as an exhaustive review of the literature, but rather as an attempt to review some of the prominent themes. As we examine these themes and how they relate to understanding, preventing, and treating burnout, we will not only highlight common ideas (or opinions) but also point out the limitations of the current literature.

As you'll see, when the literature on burnout is analyzed, it reveals the need for a comprehensive and integrated theory of burnout, encompassing personal conflicts of psychotherapists, issues in the professional's family of origin, and the environment or systems of which the therapist is a part, as well as explaining the interaction of these factors. We shall propose a comprehensive theoretical framework based on self psychology in concert with principles of general systems theory and the bridging insights of Murray Bowen. This theory takes into account both individual and social realities, which are separately describable but functionally inseparable.

A therapist who works with both individual experience and interactional forces must be able to shift focus, concentrating sometimes on the system and sometimes on the self. By alternating vantage points, the therapist can move across models to help reverse the process of burnout. Because "the system" and "the self" are only different viewpoints for describing aspects of burnout (and people's lives), one cannot separate them. Neither perspective is right or wrong, but each is more or less useful in different circumstances.

In Chapter 2 we summarize the self psychological theories of Heinz Kohut as they relate to the development of narcissistic vulnerability and how it creeps into the lives and practices of psychotherapists, making them susceptible to burnout. We also discuss the healthy rewards in the practice of psychotherapy and distinguish them from emotionally using patients. We can be affirmed by doing therapeutic work—but only when that work is a mature expression of ourselves, rather than an attempt to prop up a needy and insecure self. This fulfillment is a form of self-transcendence, a reaching beyond the self, that is similar to the creative expression of an artist.

Next we explore how difficulties in the development of the self may result in a type of therapeutic grandiosity, what has been referred to as the "God complex," and how that affects a propensity towards burnout. It turns out that defensive strategies to deny patients' attempts to look up to and lean on their therapists—often by reducing therapy to a friendly encounter between peers—is not the expression of democratic spirit, but an unwillingness to bear the weight of the patients' need to idealize us in order to draw strength for themselves.

In Chapter 3 we explore the constraints and possibilities of the systems of which every therapist is a part. When these systems function smoothly we hardly notice their complex effect on our lives. Unfortunately, however, when they don't—and we're caught up in dysfunctional organizations—we're more likely to notice the debilitating effect such circumstances have on us than to recognize the systematic forces at work.

Burnout reverberates in the present but resonates with the past. At any one time, a person may be grappling with narcissistic vulnerability, the peculiar demands inherent to the practice of psychotherapy, unresolved family issues played out in the workplace, pressures from home, a phase of life crisis (such as the birth of a child or a marital separation), and a demeaning bureaucracy. We will show how psychotherapists get caught up in a variety of destructive feedback loops—and suggest ways to keep that from happening.

In Chapter 4, we offer an integration of the various ideas we have been developing from self psychology and from systems theory. Overly ambitious strivings complicated by the God complex, often reinforced by the pressure of patients' emotional needs, frequently lead to intensified therapist effort and escalating patient demands and expectations, all within the context of declining family support and understanding. The psychotherapist works harder to recruit and maintain a self-sustaining milieu, drifting even further away from his or her family. Family members become increasingly angry and distant.

Then, in the final three chapters, we turn our attention to prevention and treatment—how to keep helping from hurting. In Chapter 5, we discuss self-assessment, support groups, effective supervision, and creating balance in one's life. In Chapters 6 and 7 on treatment we review diagnosis, treatment options, and phases of therapy. We explore various aspects and complications of the treatment process. The image of the wounded healer provides the antidote to the psychotherapist who operates as a grandiose savior. True healers, by virtue of coping with their own suffering and remaining fully aware of their own vulnerabilities, become pilgrims with others on the path to healing. This not only provides protection against burnout but creates the possibility for finding psychotherapeutic work sustaining and invigorating.

In the final chapter, a case study, we illustrate the long-term psychotherapy of a counselor who was suffering from burnout. We have drawn from a chronological review of a twice-weekly therapy that lasted over four years.

WHEN HELPING STARTS TO HURT

1

THE BURDENS OF HELPING

At the beginning of his first counseling session, Robert, a tall, well dressed social worker in a psychotherapy group practice, slumped dejectedly into an easy chair and announced in a lifeless tone that he was burned out. He went on to describe the evolution of his career as a psychotherapist. He described how his initial enthusiastic idealism had turned into boredom and apathy. He frequently found himself distracted and inattentive with his clients, relying on superficial listening skills to get through the hour. Where once he had been passionately committed to his career, working long hours, he now found himself watching the clock and daydreaming of bass fishing in Maine. He spoke of the dread of taking on a new client, feeling that he'd heard it all before. He was tired of hearing about all the tragedy and sorrow in people's lives and was losing confidence in his ability to help them. More and more he found himself telling clients about his own experiences. At first he told himself that he was becoming more open and sharing his own stories as useful examples. Then one day a client objected, "Why are you telling me about your life?" The truth was that

Robert had grown less and less able to tolerate the one-sided nature of the helping relationship. In addition, he didn't have anybody but his clients to talk with about his dilemma.

His wife Ann, five years younger than he, had gone back to work two years earlier as a buyer for a department store so that they would have more money for their children's college education. Their son and daughter, now teenagers, were rarely at home and expressed less and less interest in doing things together as a family. Regrettably, Robert himself often felt too drained to be an active part of the family. When he turned to his wife for support, he found her angry and distant, resentful of all the years when his clients came first and he was emotionally unavailable to her and the children. Ann would frequently complain, "How come you're so understanding to all those people at work but don't seem to care about my feelings? And why don't you ever help out around here without being asked when it's obvious that things need to be done?" Robert knew she was right, but felt that more and more was being expected of him right when he had less and less to give. He needed someone to listen to him. Maybe he needed psychotherapy, or career counseling to find a new vocation.

Linda reported similar feelings to Robert's. She had worked for the last six years as a supervising psychologist in a local mental health clinic. She, too, had felt her enthusiasm turn to apathy and her idealism to cynicism under the lead weight of administrative bureaucracy. Due to staff cutbacks her caseload had increased by nearly 50 percent. She was expected to improve the collection rate among the therapists she supervised, despite their deep-seated aversion to setting or collecting fees of any kind. After all, how do you charge for caring? Moreover, Linda was responsible for promulgating and enforcing new state mandated record-keeping requirements that were far more burdensome and restrictive than previous regulations. In the background, her agency was experiencing a serious problem with an unusually rapid turnover among secretarial support staff.

The position of clinic director had been vacant for nine months and remained unfilled. As a result of all this pressure, Linda's work had become perfunctory and meaningless, as had her marriage. She took solace in her presentations at professional meetings and in an affair she maintained with a psychologist in another state whom she had met during one of her professional workshops. She sought therapy to deal with her feelings of depletion and a sense that, apart from the affair, her life was flat, empty, and meaningless.

Both Robert and Linda could be said to be experiencing professional burnout, a painful erosion of the spirit in response to the pressures of work and an insufficiently sustaining personal life. Unfortunately, the term burnout has become so familiar as to take on the status of a cliche and is sometimes spoken of dismissively, perhaps as a way of distancing ourselves from the intense pain and disillusion experienced by people like Robert and Linda. But their pain is very real.

To understand burnout and the tremendous toll it takes on the lives of men and women in the helping professions, let's begin by examining how this condition has been defined and what some of its causes are.

DEFINITIONS AND SYMPTOMS

While the term burnout was originally used in the 1960s to refer to the effects of chronic drug abuse, Herbert J. Freudenberger, a New York City psychoanalyst, is generally credited with first applying the concept to the problem of occupational exhaustion among those in the helping professions. One of his early articles (1974) on burnout described the phenomenon of burnout among volunteer workers in community social service agencies. He described a variety of symptoms in these workers, noting that charisma and commitment were gradually replaced by exhaustion, fatigue, and other psychosomatic ailments. Previously competent workers began to doubt not only their powers to heal but also their powers to lead. Freudenberger saw the phenomenon of burnout as a risk experienced by the dedicated and highly committed, who struggle both with inner pressure to accomplish and succeed and with external pressure to serve the needs of unhappy people who frequently bring to treatment overwhelming dilemmas. Freudenberger defined burnout as "a state of fatigue or frustration brought about by devotion to a cause, way of life, or relationship that failed to produce the expected reward" (Freudenberger, 1980, p. 13).

Since Freudenberger, a great number of definitions of burnout have been proposed. While these definitions have slight variations, most are some variation of Freudenberger's definition. He emphasized two important points about burnout. The first is that it isn't just exhaustion from overwork; it is not something that can be cured by taking a vacation. Burnout isn't just tiredness. It is, as we said, an erosion of the spirit. It is important to realize that burnout is not just a condition of the body, but also of the soul. It involves a loss of faith in the very enterprise of helping.

The second point is that while burnout can occur in many fields, it seems particularly prevalent in the helping professions. Essentially, all the definitions state that burnout is a state of fatigue or emotional disillusion in those involved in people-related work who begin with high ideals and commitment, where this vision has been replaced by disillusion or even cynicism. Finally, even though the term burnout has become so familiar that we take it for granted, something important is captured in its metaphoric image. The tragedy of burnout is that its victims start out with such bright hopes.

Ayala Pines (1993) differentiates burnout from stress, in that, while many people experience stress, only those who entered their professions with high ideals and motivation can experience burnout. Again, notice the emphasis on a gradual depletion of the spirit and a loss of faith in our capacity to make a difference in a generous calling. These factors suggest a tension between the claims of individual fulfillment and the claims of caring for others. Does benevolent concern for others somehow detract from, rather than express, our own enlightened self-interest? These are some of the questions we'll consider as we go along.

Burnout has physiological, behavioral, psychological, and spiritual features (see Table 1). Physical symptoms may include fatigue and physical depletion, irritability, gastrointestinal disturbances, headaches, back pain, weight loss, and sleeplessness. Behavioral symptoms include coming late to work, working long hours but accomplishing little, loss of enthusiasm, quickness to frustration and anger, boredom, becoming increasingly rigid, and difficulty making decisions. Behavioral symptoms commonly have interpersonal features, such as withdrawal from colleagues, closing out new input, and increased irritation with coworkers. Another symptom is a growing dependence on alcohol, drugs, or some other means to anesthetize oneself and soothe the daily pain of spiritual erosion.

Psychological features of burnout include depression, emptiness, increasingly negative self-concept, as well as negative attitudes towards work, life, and other people. Psychological symptoms may also include guilt, self-blame for not accomplishing more with clients, or, at times, the other extreme of feelings of omnipotence. Spiritual features include loss of faith, meaning, and purpose. There can be a crisis of values, heightened scrupulosity, or changes in religious ideas and affiliations. There may be feelings of despair, as in low spirits (or dark night of the soul), alienation and estrangement. Other symptoms are lack of inspiration, courage, and vitality.

In addition to these physiological, behavioral, psychological, and spiritual symptoms, burned-out professionals may also become increasingly cynical towards clients and blame them for their own difficulties. This in turn may lead to derogatory labels, where clients are too quickly labeled "borderline" or "character disordered." Obviously, not all professionals who are suffering burnout experience all of these feelings; more commonly, some combination of symptoms is evident. Too

TABLE 1
Symptoms of Burnout

Physiological	Behavioral	Psychological	Spiritual	Clinical
Fatigue	Loss of enthusiasm	Depression	Loss of faith	Cynicism towards clients
Physical depletion	Coming late to work	Emptiness	Loss of meaning	Day dreaming during sessions
Irritability	Accomplishing little despite long hours	Negative self-concept	Loss of purpose	Hostility towards clients
Headaches	Quickness to frustration and anger	Pessimism	Feelings of alienation	Boredom towards clients
Gastrointestinal disturbances	Becoming increasingly rigid	Guilt	Feelings of estrangement	Quickness to diagnose
Back pain	Difficulty making decisions	Self-blame for not accomplishing more	Despair	Quickness to medicate
Weight change	Closing out new input	Feelings of omnipotence	Changes in values	Blaming clients
Change in sleep pattern	Increased dependence on drugs		Changes in religious beliefs	
	Increased withdrawal from colleagues		Change in religious affiliation	
	Irritation with co-workers			

often professionals beginning to experience these powerful feelings see only one way out of a bleak situation, leaving their chosen profession.

Unfortunately, burnout is too often defined only by its symptoms. As a result, many helping professionals do not recognize the problem until burnout has reached an advanced state. While it is difficult to delineate precise stages of burnout, the early phase is often mistaken for simple tiredness or low energy or boredom. Not until burnout has reached a more advanced stage, where the symptoms are more prominent, is burnout usually recognized. Even at this point it is often diagnosed only because of a poor performance evaluation that has created a crisis, or because of physiological symptoms that have become acute, or because of interpersonal problems. Rarely do professionals present for treatment of burnout as the primary issue.

Many of the symptoms of burnout, including loss of enthusiasm, tardiness, and guilt were manifested in Charles, a third-year psychiatric resident. Yet he continued driving himself to work harder, assuming that the discouragement he was feeling was just a stage in the learning process. He kept at bay the darker thought that he just might not be cut out for a career in psychiatry. Eventually, however, he confided to his supervisor that he was bitterly disappointed with the lack of progress of his patients, and admitted that he may have prescribed medication too quickly, in order to feel that he was doing something. After talking for a while, he confided that he was disillusioned with the effectiveness of psychotherapy and found himself working longer and longer hours trying to keep up with his unrealistic expectations, while becoming less and less productive. As a result of his Sisyphean efforts, he was constantly tired, and yet he had difficulty sleeping. His mid-rotation evaluation was barely adequate, and the clinic director noted that Charles had become extremely defensive in supervision. He seemed oddly relieved by this evaluation, because now he was able to admit that he was questioning his longtime dream of becoming a psychiatrist. "If I can't even take care of myself, how can I be of any use to my patients?"

While Charles had been showing many of the symptoms of burnout for months, it was not until the negative evaluation revealed the deficiencies in his performance that the extent of his burnout emerged. His case illustrates two important points about burnout: First, its effects are insidious and often hidden (even from the sufferer) until the problem is far advanced, and second, burnout is particularly a problem in the helping professions because therapists and other counselors often need years of training and practice to be competent enough to have an impact on their clients. Having an impact, and sensing that one does, is crucial to career satisfaction. Jobs that allow active, skillful involvement that produces tangible results are inherently sustaining and rewarding. Therapy and counseling, unfortunately, are basically passive and controlled; what tangible results are achieved are often long and slow in coming. What's more, successful outcome often occurs after the helping relationship has been terminated, and ironically, therapists are only likely to hear again from clients who failed to accomplish what they set out to do.

Instead of working actively and seeing positive results of their labors, helping professionals must suspend their own urge to act in order to listen in silence for long hours. Listening, a strenuous but silent activity, means that therapists must for extended periods of time serve as containers for their clients' unhappy feelings. Ultimately, the skillful therapist does accomplish something and does see results. But since this process involves a protracted apprenticeship, what sustains people in learning years? Why are the most sensitive therapists in training (who often have the potential to be the best therapists) the ones most likely to question their efficacy? Why do some good young therapists give up and others become gradually depleted? These questions go to the heart of what causes burnout.

Karen, a nurse working in a private psychiatric hospital, was in the early throes of burnout. Having endured a painful divorce three years earlier, Karen was living with her seven-year-old daughter. She commuted 45 minutes to work in a 15-year-old Plymouth, badly in need of repairs. Since the divorce, she had dated very little and had little social life. She sought therapy to reduce flare-ups of migraine and symptoms of spastic colitis, which had developed over the previous year. When speaking about her job on an adolescent unit, she frequently employed the term "borderline" and characterized the patients as "manipulative." Recently, she had felt overwhelmed and emotionally drained after work and wondered if her irritability with other people was in some way a carryover from her attitudes toward her patients, as well as from the legacy of her failed marriage. She was beginning to question her competence as a psychiatric nurse, despite consistently glowing performance evaluations.

Karen's story illustrates another important point about burnout. Competent people can continue to perform well even while suffering.

Both Charles and Karen showed many of the symptoms of burnout that have been described. However, since the process is insidious, neither of them recognized the warning signs of burnout until it was far advanced. Charles sought relief only after he received a negative performance evaluation, which caused him to reflect more honestly on what had been happening to him. Karen sought professional help because she saw the persistence of physical symptoms as a problem. In other words, like most of us, both were slow to heed their feelings. For Charles it took a failure to achieve to make him pay attention to what was happening; for Karen, getting sick legitimized her asking for help when feeling overburdened had not. Neither came to treatment to deal specifically with burnout.

Like a lot of people, Charles and Karen took it for granted

that work is a burden. But why is that? Why do we come to think of work as an ordeal that a mature person endures uncomplainingly? Shouldn't work be a place for us to feel strong, creative, and satisfied? And if instead we feel weak, dull, and dissatisfied, why do we think of ourselves as inadequate, rather than that something must be wrong with the situation?

These case vignettes demonstrate some of the problems in defining burnout. It is relatively easy to describe the various symptoms that accompany burnout. Unfortunately, we fail to recognize the symptoms early enough in ourselves. Why are we slow to recognize burnout in ourselves? Because work is always hard. Because the process is a slow, downhill one. Because people drawn to the helping professions try to be selfless. Because we're ashamed to be accused of complaining or feeling sorry for ourselves. Because we don't want to reveal that we're not sure we're accomplishing anything. Because the ephemeral nature of psychotherapy and counseling makes it hard to recognize, much less admit, when we're not really having any real impact.

Even when burnout is diagnosed, we still do not know very much. It's easy to fall into the fallacy of believing that naming is explaining. This is in part a legacy from the medical model. If we can only make the diagnosis, we think, then the prescription will be clear.

In dealing with burnout, however, simply diagnosing does not help to explain what went wrong. Being able to list symptoms of burnout may be helpful in assisting professionals with early detection, but does very little in terms of prevention. Somehow the medical-model approach to burnout (symptoms, diagnosis, prescriptions) remains tied to the idea that occupational depletion is primarily the result of overwork—in which case, of course, the primary cure is working less and relaxing more. And since that simple solution turns out to be impossible for most Americans (for reasons having to do with economic and personality dispositions), it remains an elusive and untested possibility. In fact, as we shall see, the reasons for burnout are far more complicated than simple overwork. Understanding some of the underlying causes of burnout is essential.

CAUSES OF BURNOUT

Describing the symptomatology of burnout in professions such as social work, pastoral counseling, chaplaincy, marriage and family therapy, psychology, psychiatry, and psychiatric nursing is far easier than understanding its underlying causes. Nevertheless, the literature on burnout reveals a number of hypotheses.

Three themes emerge. The first suggests that something within the psyche or personality of the professional produces a propensity towards burnout. The second is that burnout arises out of systemic or environmental factors; that is, the problem is in the system. A third theme looks at the interaction between psyche and system and what in that interaction may produce burnout.

Incidentally, it may seem obvious that, like any other human problem, professional burnout involves personal and situational factors, and the interaction between them. But this is rarely obvious to those actually suffering from burnout or to those trying to help them. The people directly involved are very apt to look only at one side of this equation, often the side that involves less conflict for them, and unfortunately may be the less important place to look.

Intrapsychic Contributions to Burnout

Freudenberger (1974, 1980) was one of the first to identify some of the intrapsychic or personality factors leading to burnout. He suggested that the overly dedicated and excessively committed individual is most prone to burnout. His first article was based on experiences with volunteers in a community agency. According to Freudenberger, excessively dedicated professionals tend to overextend themselves as a result of their idealism and high expectations. They take on too much and feel a tremendous pressure to succeed. If they aren't careful, they may use their work as a substitute for a social life. When this happens, there is an even greater tendency towards burnout.

Freudenberger (1974) identified another variable that might lead to burnout. Individuals who enter the field of psychotherapy not only to express themselves creatively while developing a craft and to help people put the broken pieces of their lives back together, but also to see some tangible evidence of such healing while earning a decent income, may find that their career does not live up to their lofty expectations. At the same time they may feel drained by the emotional pressure of the work. Finally, Freudenberger suggested that the burned-out therapist tends to be perfectionistic, compulsive, and achievement-oriented, and may be a loner who has a difficult time communicating his or her needs to significant others.

From Freudenberger onward, a number of writers have implicated several personality variables in the evolution of burnout. These include high idealism, high expectations, fear of success, the type-A personality, as well as developmental considerations involving unresolved issues from childhood and adulthood.

Self-esteem, which is powerfully affected by one's sense of creative effectance at work, may be one of the most important contributing factors to burnout (Allen, 1979). The person who feels actively and creatively involved in work, and believes that she is accomplishing something, will naturally feel better about herself. Creative and effective work is one of the most basic human fulfillments. But another factor that makes burnout so prevalent and so insidious is that what looks like effective performance to others may not feel that way to the professional herself. Internal expectations play an important role in setting standards that one must live up to in order to *feel* successful, and such standards, as we all know, are notoriously often unrealistically high. However, from the perspective of psychoanalytic writers (Allen, 1979), unconscious conflicts about success place the individual in a double bind. Careers may be neurotically wrecked, according to this theory, either because success is supposed to compensate for unresolved childhood disappointments, such as those related to sibling rivalry, or because success represents a forbidden oedipal victory. While this may sound far-fetched to those outside of the psychoanalytic tradition, consider the woman who became distraught because a young, attractive, newly hired female staff worker was given an office with a slightly bigger window and more square footage than hers. Or the man who is unaccountably anxious about telling the boss about being invited to speak or having a paper accepted for publication. Thus, far from being a simple matter of overwork, burnout is related to feeling that one has fallen short of one's goals and aspirations, internal standards which, on the one hand, may be impossibly high and, on the other, impossibly conflicted. No wonder burnout is such a tenacious process.

Adult developmental considerations may also be a factor in burnout. Farber (1983), for example, referring to the work of Erikson, Levinson, and Valliant, suggests that life events at certain stages may significantly affect one's ability to tolerate stress and to work effectively. Midlife issues, for example, might involve a reexamination of life's meaning, as well as a growing dissatisfaction with one's marriage or role as a partner and a struggle to continue to be generative. Obviously, attempting to deal with such midlife issues while continuing to treat needy clients is draining. Midlife issues may leave one feeling flat and restless at work, dreaming of taking up sailing. Consider, for example, the 35-year-old social worker who decides to divorce because she is tired of submerging herself in her marriage, and then finds that she cannot make a creative change at work because of the additional financial and emotional pressures of being a single parent. Or the academic psychiatrist who at the age of 40 decides to try to spend more time with his family, while at the same time he is feeling more pressure at work due to his upcoming consideration for tenure. In both of these examples developmental factors interact with career issues in a way that may produce burnout.

Suran and Sheridan (1985) also stress developmental considerations in understanding burnout. Borrowing from Erikson's stage theory, they propose four stages of professional development: (1) identity versus role confusion, (2) competence versus inadequacy, (3) productivity versus stagnation, and (4) rededication versus disillusionment. This model seeks to describe essential tasks that must be mastered at each level in the move towards professional competence. Through each of these stages there are both professional and personal tasks that need to be mastered. In this model burnout is the result of unresolved conflicts and tasks that have not been mastered as therapists make their way through these stages.

In addition to developmental considerations, cognitive appraisal of stressors, developmental or otherwise, can play a central role in burnout (Farber, 1983). From this perspective, stress is exacerbated by the individual perception and cognitive appraisal of threat. For example, people who work long hours with high caseloads but who perceive some control over their hours and are appropriately rewarded and valued for their work will most likely perceive stress much differently from coworkers who work the same hours but don't feel valued or properly rewarded. There is a big difference between doing extra work because you *want* to and doing it because you *have* to.

The ways in which one views stress and attempts to reduce it are important factors in the development of burnout. William James (1902) anticipated this in his lectures in 1901–1902 when he talked about "healthy mindedness," which he saw as the ability to view things in a basically optimistic way. While it is obvious that cognitive appraisal of stress plays an important role in understanding burnout, the theory does not explain why some people are able to view "stressful" situations in a way that enables them to feel positive, while others view the same situations quite differently. Basic questions are left unanswered; underlying factors must still be teased out, since they influence cognitive appraisal. Part of the answer may lie in the connection between cognitive and developmental factors. Thus, if significant life events have reduced one's ability to handle stress, then one's cognitive outlook may lead to burnout and reduced job satisfaction. While this seems to make good theoretical sense, there are still unanswered questions. Again, some are able to handle developmental stress and maintain points of view that prevent burnout, while some are not. All the attempts to view things positively and stay optimistic begin to wear thin if one's work environment takes more than it gives or if life events have been so draining that one has few emotional resources left.

Another personality factor that may underlie burnout is related to "nonreciprocated attentiveness," the giving that is an essential part of the psychotherapeutic context (Berkowitz, 1987). While therapists may expect stress and difficulty to be part of their therapeutic relationships, they are frequently not prepared for the lack of expressed appreciation from their clients. Constant giving in a one-way relationship, without feedback or perceived success, is hard on anybody. But some people apparently have a much more difficult time than others sustaining the nonreciprocated attentiveness that is a part of the psychotherapeutic relationship. We might speculate that these are people who go into helping primarily to gain gratitude, people with a high need to be admired or people who depend on external praise to let them know they're headed in the right direction. Some people become therapists not so much to help people as to get people to like them.

Many idealistic mental health professionals bring to the profession unrealistic expectations in terms of "curing" people (as though unhappiness were like an infection treatable with antibiotics), of working conditions, of other staff, of themselves, of their new roles, and of client growth (Friedman, 1985; Kestenbaum, 1984; Raider, 1989; Stevenson, 1989). How many in the mental health field began with the fantasy of being able to cure hurting people while joined with other mental health professionals committed to building a warm, accepting, supportive, holding environment, in offices furnished with quiet elegance? Obviously, the harsh reality of clients with long-term chronic problems, difficult colleagues, some of whom seem more troubled than the clients they treat, and dingy offices with hand-me-down furniture can quickly destroy the fantasy. When professionals have expectations that are too high, they may push themselves to accomplish too much and then become proud of the exhaustion which accompanies their work, thereby setting the stage for burnout. This drivenness may also be related to the new roles that therapists are being given due to the status of their position, which may then result in their struggling to live up to new goals and expectations.

Unrealistic expectations may be especially manifested in terms of expectations of client growth. The same urge to help and to be seen as helpful that propels many into the therapeutic professions often fosters grandiose notions of completely turning people's lives around, even when that may not be possible, not to mention unnecessary or unwanted. Too often, when clients come in with specific problems, their therapists believe that they should reorganize their lives or root out ancient problems. Great expectations on the part of the therapist with regard to client growth not only interfere with the process of psychotherapy but may also lead to burnout. If the therapist needs clients to change, he or she is in trouble. On the one hand, the client will most likely feel the pressure of the therapist to get well, as a way of making the therapist feel better. Compassion is thus interpreted as pressure. On the other hand, if the client does not get better, the therapist may feel ineffective and frustrated. In this case therapeutic failure may be a cognitive problem; that is, the growth of the client may not match the expectations held by the therapist. Most therapists would agree that the responsibility for change belongs to the client and that the therapist's role is to be a catalyst for change.

Yet knowing this does little to modify the high expectation level of many therapists.

The high expectations of the therapist may also be a function of unconscious grandiosity or excessive narcissism. R. Friedman (1985) mentions that the frustration of omnipotent wishes was listed as a problem by a number of psychiatrists he studied. He notes that therapists have a great need to help and at times to rescue others. When that need is thwarted, they often feel quite frustrated. This might be understood as a frustration of the therapist's grandiosity or narcissism, here defined as any function or mental activity that serves to maintain self-esteem. For many therapists the need to be needed is an overly important source of well-being.

The psychotherapist's emotional inadequacies or fragile self-esteem, frequently manifested in a narcissistic style, may be a factor in a number of other ways (Welt & Herron, 1990). Fragile narcissism may make the therapist particularly vulnerable to certain types of clients. For example, more than likely, ungrateful and hostile clients will provide little or no reinforcement of the therapist's self-esteem; in fact, frequently they will leave vulnerable therapists feeling drained. Clients who respond to attempts at empathic interpretation with comments such as, "It's a good thing you think you know what I'm feeling, because I sure don't think you do," or "I wish you would say something helpful," do not exactly bolster one's confidence. Too often, instead of attempting to understand and interpret negative transference or a misunderstanding on the part of hostile patients, the narcissistically vulnerable therapist works even more diligently to win their gratitude. This may lead to extending the session beyond the 45–50-minute norm in an attempt to be more helpful. This in turn makes the therapist late for the next session or further behind on paperwork, leaving him feeling like he is always running but never getting anywhere (like a hamster on a treadmill). Eventually, therapists insecure in their skills and dependent on clients to like them may avoid taking on angry or assertive clients and seek instead to fill their caseloads with dependent and compliant ones. Therapists may not bring about significant change with such people, but at least the clients won't give them a hard time.

The therapist who struggles with feelings of inadequacy and insecurity, and who needs to be liked by his or her clients, may have great difficulty with boundaries. While most therapists know intellectually about the need for clear and consistent boundaries with clients, their emotional needs sometimes overwhelm their good judgment. For example, sessions may be extended for certain clients, fees may be unnecessarily reduced, and telephone contacts may become extensive, all as a way of being seen in a more positive light.

Jim, for example, a psychologist in private practice, routinely let sessions run longer than the 50-minute hour he scheduled and so would frequently find himself harried by the end of a day, as he got further and further behind. He would take telephone calls from clients at night and routinely schedule sessions at inconvenient times to accommodate difficult clients. He felt put upon and taken advantage of. What he didn't realize, however, was that he allowed, even encouraged, these excessive pressures on his time. Feeling inadequate about the quality of therapy he did provide made him feel guilty and reluctant to confront (or even say no to) his clients' needs for attention outside the hour. As a result, Jim felt tired, stale—and worse, increasingly angry and irritated at his clients. His need to be liked kept him from holding to important boundaries, which in turn left him more and more exhausted and drained.

Jim's dilemma captures one of the central ironies of the helping professions, which involve doing for a living the kinds of things (listening, being empathic) that people usually do out of love and friendship. Thus, there is in the helping professions something inherently suggestive of personal relationships. Perhaps that's why William Schofield called psychotherapy *The*

Purchase of Friendship (1964). For the client, the helping relationship allows deep yearnings to emerge, yearnings for understanding, love, maybe sometimes even punishment or perhaps sexual fulfillment. But what about the helper? Doesn't the same intimate and personal situation stir personal longings in him or her? A climate of caring suggests mutual exchange. That the helping relationship is designed to be one-way and that powerful sanctions are in place to keep it that way doesn't mean the pressures to turn a professional relationship into something else cease to exist, or that resisting them for years doesn't cause a strain.

Perhaps the most blatant abuse of boundaries occurs when therapists become sexually involved with their clients. In these cases the therapist is able to convince him or herself that the attraction is both real and mutually beneficial to both parties and the obvious transference and countertransference issues are conveniently ignored. While we justifiably experience outrage at these abuses of power, perhaps part of our outrage and anger is a defensive reaction to our own deep awareness of similar temptations. Again, these abuses happen slowly, as boundaries are allowed to become more ambiguous over a period of time. They speak not necessarily to the abusive natures of such therapists but rather to the deep emotional emptiness and depletion that come with the process of burnout. Thus, despite the obvious psychological damage that may result from such liaisons, and the fact that they violate all professional ethical standards (not to mention possible malpractice and criminal liability), the reality is that such violations are an unfortunate attempt to feed the inadequacies and depletion of the therapist. The grandiose self of the therapist is mirrored in such liaisons, with the tragic result that all of the implications are frequently not examined. Obviously, this is a serious problem in the mental health professions. What is frequently missed is the power of the archaic narcissism that motivates such behavior. Most professionals do not intentionally violate boundaries. Their own needs to be admired, liked, or idealized, along with simple emotional exhaustion, cause them to become more ambiguous in their boundary definitions.

Burnout isn't simply the result of too much work, but also a measure of the gratification we receive from our work. In fact, it is precisely this lack of satisfaction that often drives helping professionals to blur the boundaries between themselves and their clients, as they anxiously hope to get something more (other than professional gratification) out of the relationship. Most professional groups have very strict ethical guidelines which absolutely forbid sexual relations with clients. Yet, many other difficult areas remain. Professional guidelines forbid dual relationships with clients, as another boundary violation. Some therapists, in their need to be liked and needed, become friends with their clients, or join business ventures with clients, or even barter services for therapy. One therapist felt bad about a client's difficulty paying for therapy, and so made a deal which allowed his client to do plumbing repairs at his home as a way of covering the cost of therapy. What about a therapist collaborating with a client on a book or series of videos? What about the senior clinician who provides both supervision and therapy to the same client, or the professor who sees several of his students for psychotherapy? All of these are boundary violations that grow out of vulnerable professionals' own needs to be liked, idealized, and admired, which result in an abuse of the power differential in the therapeutic relationship as noted by Peterson (1992).

We believe that the issue of therapeutic narcissism ties together the various intrapsychic and personality factors that predispose professionals to burnout. In proposing this, we are well aware that narcissism or struggling with maintaining self-esteem is a universal problem. However, we frequently unconsciously pick professions in which we can attempt to meet needs that should have been met earlier in life. We may be searching for intimacy. Perhaps earlier failures to get parental attention are compensated when patients hang on our every word. As a result, psychotherapy can become one of the fields to which individuals are drawn as a way to foster a stronger sense of selfhood.

The need to receive admiring attention, which supports a vigorous sense of self, may bring one to a profession with high idealism. It may lead to grandiose expectations of client change. It may result in long hours and compromised boundaries, as one attempts to please difficult clients.

Systemic Contributions to Burnout

As professionals we like to think of ourselves as autonomous individuals, but we are embedded in networks of relationships that define us and sustain us. We know this, of course, about our clients, but we often seem to forget it about ourselves. Somehow our professional educations cultivate conceptions of individualism that picture the professional helping person as finding his or her own bearings within, declaring independence from the webs of relationship which have originally formed him or her, or at least neutralizing them.

All this is not to say that we cannot be autonomous, in the sense of self-directing (knowing what we want and where we stand), or even original, in being able to think and act on our own. But we cannot leap out of the human condition and become self-sustaining, secure, and satisfied, with no need for emotional sustenance and support at work and at home. While there are many theories about personality variables in burnout, there are fewer focusing on the therapist's environment. Christina Maslach, a leading researcher in this area, summarizes the results of her work, which has led her to emphasize the power of environmental factors:

> I am forced by the weight of my research to conclude that the problem is best understood in terms of the social situational sources of job related stress. The prevalence of the phenomena and the range of seemingly desperate professionals who are affected by it suggest that the search for causes is better directed away from the unending cycle of identifying the "bad

> people" and towards uncovering the operational and structural characteristics in the "bad" situations where many good people function. (Maslach, in Daniel & Rogers, 1981, p. 233)

Several studies have suggested that the key to understanding burnout is to be found in the environments in which they work (Clark & Vaccaro, 1987; Lavandero, 1981; Raider, 1989). These environments may impose rigid work schedules or be particularly draining, as in residential treatment agencies for children. Too often unrealistic expectations are put upon workers with too little support, resulting in emotional exhaustion. In addition, organizational factors, such as occupational tedium, lack of support and adequate supervision, or even abusive supervision (Rogers, 1987; Rosenblatt & Mayer, 1975), may contribute to poor morale and burnout. Some professionals complain about a lack of proper equipment and furniture, top-heavy administration without proper support services, excessive bureaucracy and paperwork, low pay, and perhaps the greatest single contribution to professional dissatisfaction, responsibility without authority. Other factors include a high turnover of clients which may lead to the feeling that one's work is superficial, lack of positive feedback, and limited opportunity or incentive for financial reward.

Feeling powerless in one's work setting may contribute to burnout (Daniel & Rogers, 1981). Raquepaw and Miller (1989) found that psychologists working in private practice where they are their own boss have higher rates of job satisfaction than those working in agency settings, and that in private practice a high caseload produces a greater sense of therapist personal accomplishment. Many of us in not-for-profit public agencies are familiar with the impact of organizational factors in addition to the pressures of HMOs, IPAs, PPOs, and managed care.

In public clinics we are forced to deal with the high no-show rate and at the same time challenged to generate more revenue and improve the collection rate. We have witnessed the effects on morale of hiring freezes and pay freezes, not to mention cutbacks in staff. Such cutbacks, so common everywhere these days, carry a threefold burden: Less staff means more work for those who remain; staff cutbacks mean watching people we know and care about get laid off; and finally, watching others get laid off reminds us that the same thing could happen to us if we do less than everything asked of us. Whether in an agency or in private practice, most can relate to the additional pressure from massive changes in insurance reimbursement, on the one hand, and the growing competition of a variety of self-help groups, on the other. Most of us can also relate to such pressures as rising office expenses, inflation, and unemployment as they impact the practice of psychotherapy.

Many of us in the mental health field are faced with very difficult client populations. While some therapists may joke about their ideal caseload being comprised of people who don't need therapy, few of us actually get to treat many of these intelligent, introspective, upper-middle-class clients, who are interested in personal growth. Dealing with chronically mentally ill clients, who are caught in the revolving social service door, or chaotic families, who go from one crisis to another and seem to lack any strength to deal with those crises, causes a constant drain on caseworkers, coupled with a sense of very little accomplishment. Dealing with too many borderline clients, who frequently threaten suicide, or call at 2:00 a.m. "to talk," or get in trouble with the law, or want disability, leaves many professionals feeling impotent. These difficult clients are both exhausting and draining, leaving professionals feeling ineffective, tired, and wondering why they are spending so much energy with such limited success.

Many of the systemic factors that contribute to burnout are not simply the result of working in particular agencies, but may be endemic to the practice of psychotherapy (Bugental, 1990; Guy, 1987; Kottler, 1986). Spending all day listening to the intimate thoughts of clients and yet maintaining appropriate boundaries, while attempting to be empathically attuned to family and friends as well, is quite an undertaking. Whether one is in private practice or works in an agency, difficult patients can be a problem. Moreover, at times, hearing similar stories and struggles day after day leaves therapists flat and bored.

Ironically, our ability to show consideration is often less flexible at home than at work. We love our families, but that love gets strained. Conflict, habit, and the demanding pressures of professional empathizing make us less patient where patience is most needed. It's not, as we're sometimes accused, that we "care more about our clients than we do about our families," but that relationships at work are less clotted with conflict and resentment than those at home.

Burnout may also be partially related to the technique and stance of a type of psychotherapy (Cooper, 1986). The therapist is bound by a therapeutic stance that attempts to combine both compassion and distance, by the particular theory from which he or she practices, and by rules of technique such as therapeutic neutrality that stem from one's theory. The rules and theory are designed to prevent the client from rewarding the therapist, and so explicit expressions of gratitude from clients are usually interpreted as transference. When therapeutic distance is combined with isolation, therapists may find themselves bored and detached; like state-funded bureaucrats on autopilot, they may end up doing a depersonalized form of therapy and relying on superficial listening skills. In the absence of reliable outcome studies for many forms of therapy, therapists may wonder if what they are doing is even helping, rendering them skeptical of the whole occupation.

Some of the systemic factors that lead to burnout are inherent in specific mental health settings, while others are related to the practice of psychotherapy itself. Farber (1983) summarizes five of these systemic stressors, which combine in a variety of ways:

1. Nonreciprocated attentiveness, that is, the unique one-way relationship that is an essential part of the psychotherapeutic relationship.
2. Role ambiguity, where there is a lack of clarity about the criteria for success, even while one is pressured to succeed.
3. Role conflict resulting from inconsistent or incompatible demands placed on the worker. Such conflict may emerge in the form of value clashes, problems with one's supervisors, or resentment at being forced to do work outside the domain of one's expertise.
4. Role overload, as professionals encounter excessive workloads, such as increasing caseloads due to budget cutbacks and pressure to do more paperwork without adequate secretarial help.
5. Feelings of inconsequentiality, when therapists sense that, no matter how hard they work, appropriate payoffs and appreciation are not and will not be forthcoming.

After reviewing the various systemic factors that contribute to burnout, one question is left unanswered: Why do some therapists burn out while others, perhaps in the same agency, do not? In fact, some people seem to thrive on stress, while others burn out because of it. Looking at organizational and systemic factors doesn't bring us any closer to an answer to this question. The answer lies in the interaction between the self of the therapist and the system in which he or she works.

The Interaction Between Intrapsychic and Systemic Contributions to Burnout

If both personality and environmental forces contribute to emotional overload, obviously we need to look at the combination of these factors. However, it isn't just the sum of personal and systemic factors that leads to burnout; it is the particular nature of their interaction. In one formulation, for example, Daniel and Rogers (1981) suggest that burnout may result from the interaction among the therapist's ego involvement, professional expectations, and the social and economic factors within the agency.

Among many ways of looking at the interaction of psyche and system, one very useful one is suggested by the family systems theory of Murray Bowen (Bowen, 1978; Kerr & Bowen, 1988). Bowen and other multigenerational theorists (E. Friedman, 1985; Weinberg & Mauksch, 1991) contend that family-of-origin issues tend to be replayed in work environments, a systems theory variation on Freud's notion of the repetition compulsion. While not all multigenerational theorists would agree with Freud that we are unconsciously motivated to seek out contemporary situations in which to work out old dramas, most would concur that conflicts at work frequently trigger family-of-origin conflicts. An obvious example involves workers who were abused as children and are now employed in an agency that works with child abuse on a regular basis. On the positive side, these persons bring a specific sensitivity to their work. But on the down side, if they are motivated more by a need to seek personal revenge or master their own suffering than by therapeutic concern for client families, they may overidentify with victims (demonizing the adults in the family in the process), act on a retributive rather than therapeutic agenda, overextend themselves, and become hostile and aggressive with other professionals who try to work with families rather than judge and punish them. Clearly, the situation provides workers with an opportunity to work on their own personal issues as they work with abused children. When there is adequate and sensitive supervision, all may benefit; when there is not, the interaction of psyche and system may lead to exploitation and deterioration.

Psychoanalytic and family systems theorists agree that people tend to interact with others in the present in ways they learned growing up. The work environment can become an ersatz family, where old conflicts are reenacted in the present. While sometimes the interaction between family-of-origin issues and the present is obvious, as in the example above, at other times the relationship is far less clear. Weinberg and Mauksch (1991) point out that the interaction between past and present conflicts can be both linear and circular. Utilizing Bowen's theory of differentiation, they suggest that linear interactions occur when persons bring to work unresolved emotional attachment to parents and then live out these family issues at work. Currying favor with the boss or its obverse, a readiness to oppose whatever those in charge decree, is only the most obvious form such unresolved attachment can take. (This is also what Bion [1961] meant when he described how work groups get sidetracked by workers' tendency to act out *dependency*, *fight-flight* and *pairing* scripts.) Oppositionalism can also take subtler forms, such as a tendency to disparage the use of medication on the part of nonmedical staff in a medical school. Anyone whose professional behavior is predictably aimed at compliance or defiance, rather than competence, may well be acting out an ancient part. Unresolved family issues can also have a more diffuse impact; for example, if one's parents fought chronically, one may respond by becoming anxious every time there is a conflict at work.

Circular interactions occur when two or more colleagues unconsciously play out their family dynamics with each other, thereby recreating their families at work or, as Weinberg and Mauksch put it, "creating a reciprocal, self-sustaining pattern of interactions and roles" (1991, p. 234). Many variations on this theme are possible. Therapists who grew up in families where they wound up being their parents' marriage counselors, or parenting their parents, or becoming a substitute partner for one of their parents, not surprisingly come away with a type of hypervigilance, such that they have difficulty relaxing and are always trying to keep conflicts from surfacing. They quickly become peacemakers at work whenever there is a hint of tension. While this can be tiring in itself, it becomes exhausting when they become involved in circular feedback loops with other coworkers. Consider the dilemma of a caseworker who tries to "rescue" a supervisor who seems needy. In the aftermath, the boundaries do not hold up, effective supervision does not occur, and both edge closer to burnout. As family-of-origin conflicts get acted out in the work environment, compounded with the reality that work settings, like families, have specific structures, personalities, and styles of communication, the potential for burnout is dramatically increased.

Another interactional perspective looks at the goodness-of-fit between person and system, with cognitive perceptions playing a central role (Raquepaw & Miller, 1989). In this schema, burnout is seen as connected to how persons perceive themselves fitting into the work situation, in terms of job satisfaction and stressors. Rogers (1987), in further attempting to understand person-job interaction, suggests the "person-environment fit theory" as a means of assessing and evaluating the goodness-of-fit between person and environment. Since stress can be significantly exacerbated by individual perception and evaluation, one's interpretation of stressors and the coping strategies that one employs in an effort to reduce stress must be considered (Farber, 1983). Nevertheless, while cognitive appraisal of stress is important for understanding burnout, by itself it does not explain why some people are better able than others to appraise problems in a way that does not lead to burnout. The goodness-of-fit theory attempts to answer this by suggesting that the proper fit of person and environment is essential. Thus, a laid-back professional will not "fit" a high pressure work environment with type-A personality supervisors. However, an aggressive worker may also not be a good fit in that organization; he may end up competing with his supervisors. What is missing in this theory is greater depth of integration in seeking to explain how variables come together to produce burnout and why this happens with some workers but not with others.

SUMMARY

We have seen that, even though they all end in the same painful result, there are many factors that contribute to the emotional depletion of burnout. Sadly, these factors erode the very impulse that urges us into our careers in the first place: benevolent concern for others. Caring about other people, which takes shape in political justice, the relief of suffering, and the love of family and friends, is fundamental to our sense of who we are and what makes our lives hang together. Pressures that block or obscure this impulse reduce—even mutilate—us. Unfortunately, burnout does just that.

The ideal of a career in the helping professions is that it will provide us with a vehicle for balancing the claims of benevolence and the claims of individual self-expression, for it offers us the opportunity to express ourselves through helping. But this is where the danger lies. It is more difficult than we like to imagine to sustain generosity on the basis of the self-fulfillment it provides. Until recently benevolence was shored up by religious love and aspiration. In a secular professional world, how is it possible without a sense of moral obligation to sustain a basis for extending help to those who do not appeal to us, or who are especially attractive to us? Can a professional career succeed in motivating and sustaining helping relationships without a moral or spiritual dimension?

While it seems clear that the direction to move in understanding burnout is the interplay of persons and environments, much work is needed to translate this integrative ideal into specifics. A number of theories have been suggested as starting points. Some look at one or more intrapsychic factors and how they interact with variables in the work environment to produce burnout. Others focus on family-of-origin issues and how old family dramas get replayed in the work environment. Because of its cybernetic nature, this is a promising line of thinking. It allows for the integration of past and present, person and system, and also explains goodness-of-fit (or the lack of it) between professionals and their vocational systems. Other cognitive appraisal theories look more generally at notions of goodness-of-fit between person and system. The need for further integration is still apparent.

In the following chapters we outline a broader method of integrating various theories. We use Kohut's understanding of the self, and of narcissistic vulnerability in particular, to show how personality may interact with a variety of systems variables, ranging from unresolved family-of-origin conflicts to specific systems factors in the work environment. This interaction creates a series of feedback loops; caught in these, the professional may begin to perceive and react to professional challenges in a way leading to burnout.

2

THE MAKING OF A HELPER: MASKED NARCISSISM

Self psychology is uniquely relevant to our investigation of burnout because it helps us understand narcissistic development and the regulation of self-esteem. This perspective, based on the contributions of Heinz Kohut, illuminates therapist susceptibility to burnout by delineating how narcissistic vulnerability develops. Self psychology enables us to get to the heart of the matter because it addresses the deep but heretofore poorly understood longing for appreciation that drives some of us into the ground. Finding healthy ways of maintaining a strong sense of self is a prerequisite for effective functioning as a professional helper.

SELF PSYCHOLOGY AND SELFOBJECTS

The concept of selfobject is essential to understanding self psychology. But what is a selfobject?

A selfobject is neither a self nor an object, but the *subjective* aspect of a relationship that is supportive of the self. The presence or activity of an object, often another person, an idea or a cause, helps to bring forth and sustain the person's sense of self. A selfobject experience is a deeply personal one; it is a sense of connection that makes one feel known and valued. Although we're used to thinking of this connection in the language of psychology—"subjective," "intrapsychic"—ultimately, the selfobject experience has spiritual overtones. Not spiritual in the sense of religious, perhaps, but certainly in terms of relating to the spirit, not tangible, affecting the soul.

According to Thomas Moore in *Care of the Soul,* soul is revealed in our attachments and in community. Our souls need to be honored and tended. A meaningful connection beyond ourselves makes us feel whole, not just because our experience is somehow recognized, but because we are recognized in some ways as beings with soul. He aptly quotes Emily Dickinson:

> Nature and God—I neither knew.
> Yet Both so well knew me.
> They startled, like Executors
> of My identity.

Ultimately, a selfobject is an intrapsychic experience. It involves the experience of images that are necessary to uphold one's sense of self. It does not describe an interpersonal relationship as it might be viewed by an outside observer.

When a small child experiences other people from a position of normal, healthy self-interest, based on what that child needs for its growth and expansion, perhaps the maintenance of its basic security, we can say the child is relating to other people narcissistically. Mental activity is narcissistic to the degree that its function is to maintain the cohesion, stability, and positive affective coloring of the sense of self (Stolorow & Lachman, 1980, p. 26). Kohut attempts to further clarify the concept of the selfobject when he refers to the small child's use of other people:

> The expected control over such (selfobject) others is then closer to the concept of the control which a grownup expects to have

> over his own body and mind, than to the concept of the control which he expects to have over others. (1971, pp. 26–27)

To further clarify an awkward but highly useful concept, selfobjects are neither selves, independent beings in their own right, nor objects, but more like mental images; the subjective aspect of a function performed by a relationship. As such, the selfobject relationship refers to an intrapsychic experience needed for the sustenance of the self. A selfobject is that dimension of our experience of something, often another person, that relates to the thing's or person's functions in shoring up our own self (Kohut, 1984, p. 49).

The hermit who has withdrawn into the desert is not necessarily suffering from selfobject deprivation because of his apparent aloneness. Indeed, such isolation seems to allow some people to experience their relationship to religious ideas and figures with an intensity that rivals the most intimate personal selfobject responsiveness. Symbolic selfobject experiences replace for the adult the more concrete selfobject needed in infancy and childhood. Experiencing the self-evoking and self-maintaining selfobject function is something we never outgrow.

Following Wolf (1989), we can talk about a developmental line of selfobject experiences. Selfobject needs can be outlined as follows:

1. A neonate needs a self-evoking experience with a real-life person who, by providing certain tuned-in responses, functions as a selfobject for that neonate.
2. An adolescent needs a self-sustaining experience with real objects or with symbols, such as provided by the adolescent subculture in the form of speech, clothes, music, idols, and so forth, which by their availability function as selfobjects for that particular adolescent.
3. An adult needs a selfobject experience with real objects or with symbols, such as provided by art, literature, mu-

sic, religion, and ideas, which by their availability function as selfobjects for that particular adult.

The subjective aspect of a relationship to an unconscious object is mediated by a symbolic presence that provides a selfobject function (Wolf, 1989, p. 54). It is important to remember, especially for later discussions of treatment, that selfobject experiences are not objectively observable from the outside. According to Wolf:

> They are not events in an interpersonal contact and are not part of social psychology. It is an error to talk about selfobject relations either as object relations or as interpersonal relations. The interpersonal relations between persons may give rise to selfobject experiences and, inferentially, one may guess at the selfobject experiences that accompany certain relations between persons. Direct access to the selfobject experiences is only by introspection and empathy. (1989, p. 55)

Selfobjects and the Hunger for Appreciation

Kohut taught us about the uniquely human yearning for appreciation that lies behind the infinite variety of our actions. One of the major reasons people become helpers is precisely because they're looking to satisfy the longing to be appreciated. The danger, of course, is that, when the patient becomes too important for the regulation and maintenance of the therapist's self-esteem—in other words, when the patient provides a necessary selfobject function for the therapist—the patient is treated not as a self with an independent center of initiative but primarily as a person-there-for-me. While this blurring of boundaries may or may not be always obvious, this dynamic is almost always at the root of burnout.

We do not mean to imply that all psychotherapists suffer from narcissistic personality disorders; indeed, hungering for attention is a universal problem of human nature. Yet, understanding this theme and the way it is played out in the lives and practices of many therapists is enormously useful in understanding therapists' needs to use patients to bolster their self-esteem and ultimately the burnout that develops among so many mental health professionals.

> A weakened or depleted self, as well as a strong, vital self, can be seen in the changing nature of the relationship between the self and its selfobjects. Self psychology holds that self-selfobject relationships form the essence of psychological life from birth to death, that a move from dependence (symbiosis) to independence (autonomy) in the psychological sphere is no more possible, let alone desirable, than a corresponding move from a life dependent on oxygen to a life independent of it in the biological sphere. (Kohut, 1984, p. 47)

Kohut goes on to explain that a person will feel strong and resilient as long as he experiences others, "as joyfully responding to him, as available to him as sources of idealized strength and calmness, as being silently present but in essence like him, and are attuned to his needs when in need of such sustenance" (1984, p. 52).

Kohut postulated that in early development the child is frustrated by the inevitable failures of parental responsiveness. It is optimal, or "good-enough" responsiveness that confirms the child's sense of worth. Affective misattunements and failures of empathy are called selfobject failures.

Unlike Freud, who thought of the human infant's needs as primarily physical, Kohut taught that babies need the affirmation of admiring attention and the security of idealizable parents. He believed that the self was pushed by its ambitions and pulled by its ideals. Ambitions are derived from inborn talents, which, if adequately recognized and validated, will provide enough push from within or behind the self to develop initially skill, eventually pride, and ultimately enthusiasm. The loyal dedication to a set of values and ideals usually comes from an omnipotent parent, outside and above the self, who pulls the child to want the ideal. Children yearn for this type of solid connection. Ideally, if a child receives adequate mirroring, then healthy assertiveness, initiative, and ambition develop; if there are sufficient successful idealizations, then values, goals, and ideals develop.

Transmuting Internalization

If the frustration that is an inevitable result of failures of parental responsiveness is developmentally appropriate and nontraumatic, the child learns that while many needs are met, not all are. Through his or her response to this frustration, the child begins to build an experience of the self and a sense of the self as worthwhile. In *One Little Boy*, Dorothy Baruch writes:

> If a child's emotional hungers are satisfied by his mother in the helpless beginnings of life when he cannot fend for himself, then he can take in better stride the necessary denials which must be imposed on him as he grows. If he were to put the matter into words, he might say, "I get angry, yes, at big people for their forbidding me things I want. But still I know they are fundamentally with me and for me. They care about me. They proved that to me when I was small." (1952, p. 191)

Similarly, as the child experiences the caregiver leaving but then returning, he or she feels frustration and then relief and calm. If most partings are nontraumatic (not too abrupt, not too frequent, and not too prolonged) and when most comings and goings are handled with sensitivity and reassurance, the child learns to trust that the caregiver will come back. This builds an internal structure (structuralization) that is self-regulating and self-soothing, which Kohut called transmuting internalization (1971, p. 49).

As the child grows, a sense of self develops, transforming the original narcissism. The child displays emerging capacities and proudly exhibits an expanding self, modified by the limits of reality along the way. We all know how children love to show off. What we may not know is how important this is to the developing sense of self. Children show off who they are—"Look at me!"—and the powerful people they wish they were—"I'm a Ninja warrior!" Children take profound pleasure in self-expression. Kohut described the infantile grandiose-exhibitionistic self as a primary, normal, healthy state as opposed to a secondary, reactive, defensive state. If the grandiose self is subjected to optimal responsiveness from the environment, the healthy narcissism, however immature, gets transformed into more mature forms: humor, creativity, empathy, and wisdom (Kohut, 1978, p. 460).

Selfobject Failure

Along the mirroring pole or line of development, if parents or other caregivers do not provide sufficient affirmation of the self in its uniqueness and particularity, normal but still immature narcissism becomes entombed in unmodified form. When the parents fail in this regard only occasionally, the child is weaned from dependence and forced to develop his or her own resources. If there are excessive failures, and the child is abruptly cut off from narcissistic supplies, the unresponded-to self is not able to transform childish grandiosity into reliable self-esteem. A narcissistic disturbance develops based on the failure of the archaic narcissism to be transformed into a more mature form. A primitive (largely unconscious) omnipotent grandiosity is perpetuated and any threat to this sense of self becomes experienced as a threat to one's very existence. Consider the following example.

Max, a 27-year-old psychology graduate student seeking psychotherapy, was raised in a military family and lived in several countries. His chief complaint was, "I want to work on the 10 percent of me that I'm dissatisfied with." Although the clinic had a sliding fee scale, he argued for the minimum fee because "a psychiatry resident would be able to learn a lot from me."

Max was a tall, thin, gawky young man with stringy, shoulder-length hair. When asked about the 10 percent, he said, "I'm driven by my genitals." He was worried about his studies because he was spending so much time looking for dates and going to parties. A major theme in his therapy was his feeling like a stranger or an alien. He frequently had the experience of being "from a different land."

During the course of Max's therapy, we learned that he was consumed by profound feelings of inferiority and inadequacy. He felt largely ignored by his mother, who was plagued and absorbed with medical problems. Even though he was an only child, Max got very little of her attention. He was angry and disappointed in his father, who was frequently abusive to his mother and critical and impatient with him. Behind his father's army bravado, he could see basic insecurity and fear of failure. Several times his father had been overlooked for promotions in rank and instead relocated to another part of the globe. The family would follow, uprooted again. Max became a peace activist and excelled academically in college, majoring in psychology and philosophy. He was looking for some kind of anchoring experience, whether in the world of ideas or in the realm of relationships. During the course of psychotherapy it came out that Max was also looking for love through sex. He had a long history of difficulty establishing trusting, meaningful relationships at an emotional level. Understandably, he had come to expect that relationships would not last. He had allowed the reception of his male genitality to substitute for the experience of a more embracing humanness (the 10 percent).

The helping professions are not, of course, the only place where people like Max with unmet narcissistic needs end up, but these professions are especially attractive to them. Those of us who never got enough sympathy and attention crave it and are hesitant to ask for it (because we're ashamed of our needs).

One way to avoid the terrible sin of being "selfish" is to be "selfless"—to seek appreciation by being helpful. Many people are hesitant to ask for attention because they learned as children to secure favor by being attentive to the needs of a parent. Take, for example, the woman who was afraid to upset her mother, who was preoccupied with tending to her sick father. Or the man who watched with mounting anxiety all the distress his assertive, demanding older brother caused his parents. Moreover, the normal needs of children may have come to represent burdens and excessive demands in the eyes of an already overburdened or precariously-put-together parent. These children's needs didn't count; there was no room for them. Their feelings may have been repeatedly invalidated. They learned, therefore, to take the listening role in relationships. Afraid to show their own needs more directly, they found intimacy by attending to the needs and feelings of others. Unfortunately, these now-grown children pay a price, as will their patients, if they choose a helping profession and practice it based on trying to satisfy unacknowledged, hidden, or masked needs of their own.

According to Swiss analyst Alice Miller:

> It is not less our fate than our talent which enables us to exercise the profession of psycho-analyst tolerating the knowledge that, to avoid losing the loved object, we were compelled to gratify our parents' unconscious needs at the cost of our own self-realization. It also means being able to experience the rebellion and mourning aroused by the fact that our parents were not available to fulfill our primary narcissistic needs. (1979, p. 54)

It is really only after we have been able to face the truth about ourselves and what we missed out on when we were small that we're able to abandon the hope, for practical purposes, of finding that ideal mother (unconsciously, of course) in another person, even a patient.

NARCISSISM AND THE MENTAL HEALTH PROFESSIONAL

Many psychotherapists were sensitive and alert children who learned quickly to adapt to the basic needs of their parents. They were then able to give their mothers (or fathers) all the attention and mirroring that the parents themselves missed as children. As a consequence, these children's own inner programs or blueprints were not allowed to develop. The ultimate outcome is narcissistic vulnerability and repeated attempts as adults to find an "ideal mother" in their own children, partners, or patients.

The narcissistically vulnerable therapist, craving admiration and appreciation, may take on an ever expanding caseload of needy and dependent patients. Ironically, such therapists often become dependent themselves on the selfobject functions performed by their patients. Consider those patients in your own practice whom you especially look forward to seeing or miss when they cancel. Think of the VIP patient who gives you a surge of self-esteem because she elected to see you for her therapy.

In the category of legitimate therapist satisfaction is the feeling of competence that accrues when a patient responds dramatically to an accurate and timely interpretation. When we say that patients become selfobjects, we use this term to describe the function associated with confirming the therapist's inner experience of self-worth.

Valerie, a short, slightly overweight administrative assistant and pastor's wife, told her therapist, Mark, a 26-year-old single psychology intern, that she imagined he was a 40-year-old married father with at least ten years of experience. Every week she complained about her husband and often made some comment to the effect that unlike her husband Mark was a sensitive, understanding man. She would say things like, "I know you understand these things but my husband doesn't." One day she blurted out how amazed she was at his extraordinary warmth and sensitivity and that she would love to go out with him if they were free to do so. On another occasion she speculated that he was very well read and figured he had read the entire collected works of Sigmund Freud. Furthermore, she "just knew" he enjoyed classical music as much as she did. Mark felt flattered and a little flustered. Disconcerted, he tried to correct her exaggerated idea of him, saying things like, "Actually I don't know too much about that. You probably know more about that than I do." He told himself that he was being honest, that he was challenging the patient's one-down position. But actually he was feeling the pressure of being used as an idealized selfobject, and instead of listening and tolerating the strain, he's actively asserting himself, acting in a very human, but not very therapeutic way.

Besides illustrating a patient who leaves her therapist feeling appreciated and respected (allowing for credulity), this case example also reminds us of the pitfalls and complications that arise from such transferences. It illustrates what Kohut described as an alterego or twinship transference, as well as some aspects of an idealizing transference.

The young therapist's self-esteem was bolstered by the "extraordinary warmth and sensitivity" comment and by Valerie's affirmation of his masculinity. On the other hand, he was quite uncomfortable about her more discrepant and inflated views of him. He also felt a sexual tension with her, e.g., he noticed her rich perfume. He felt stirred up by her in a sexual way. Such feelings may be taboo and embarrassing to a therapist, but they are after all easier to be conscious of than the feeling of being used as a selfobject. That's what was really disconcerting to him. He'd been trained to offer support by saying encouraging things to patients, building them up. And so her need to admire and look up to him—to use him as someone to look up to and draw strength from—disconcerted him, because she needed to relate to him as someone different from the person he felt himself to be.

Mark's dilemma is precisely what's so difficult about being used as a selfobject. The person using you may in the process distort the self you feel yourself to be. No doubt women feel some of the same uncanny discomfort when men relate to them as sex objects. Many therapists feel the activation of their grandiosity which emerges from being idealized as well as the need to vigorously defend against its emergence, to be one of the most difficult challenges of doing psychotherapy. In fact, we believe that the difficulty many therapists have with being idealized is rooted in their own thwarted narcissistic (self) development.

Among clergy we have observed a common masochistic defense against the emergence of the omnipotent grandiosity: "I shouldn't expect (or demand) anything for myself, but rather, my satisfaction must come from my giving others what they need (being all things to all people)." The demands of the unconscious grandiose self drain off the energy needed for further maturation and development. Thus, when the clergyperson is unable to make the congregation respond with love, the self is then threatened. You can imagine how exhausting this effort can be. The more the minister is drawn into the pastoring as a way to be loved, and at the same time denies any right to appreciation, the more effort will be required. Caught in this conflict he will be less free to do what is really needed or required based on the true needs of the congregation. How can doing a job ever be good enough if love is the real agenda?

One of the reasons we have "speaking anxiety" is because, in our desire to be loved, we forget that the primary purpose of a talk is to communicate something. If giving a talk means submitting to judgment about the very value of the self, then it's worth worrying.

If we are largely motivated out of a desire to be liked, then (a) it's hard to risk saying the hard things people sometimes need to hear, and (b) helping people change becomes secondary to making them like us. In other words, it becomes difficult or impossible to be effective as a psychotherapist. We admire some famous therapists, including Salvador Minuchin, Richard Chessick, Betty Carter, and Olga Silverstein, at least in part because they don't seem controlled by the need to make patients like them.

Narcissistic vulnerability may drive both men and women to workaholism, but there are some gender differences. Research (Chodorow, 1978; Gilligan, 1982; Miller, 1976; Notman & Nadelson, 1991) suggests that success for a man is likely to mean personal achievement, while for a woman success is often tied to feeling accepted and having successful relationships. There may be less gender discrepancy among psychotherapists than in the general population, however, since male therapists tend to score high on the femininity scale of the MMPI and to show nurturing or maternal qualities. Much of the caring shown by therapists of both genders may derive from a need to please originating from a sense of personal inadequacy and powerlessness.

If female therapists are more concerned than their male counterparts with doing things for other people, this could be a double-edged sword. On the one hand, they may be especially sensitive to clients' needs; on the other, they may become dependent on clients for narcissistic gratification. At the same time, they may be facing the typical challenges of working mothers in our society—juggling the demands of children and work. As they dutifully "feed" clients, children, and husband, female psychotherapists may find themselves drained and empty.

The Search for Selfobject Experiences

When things don't turn out for us as well as we would like (when do they ever?), we seek selfobject experiences to protect and maintain whatever level of self-functioning we have achieved. Some very empty and unfulfilled therapists even lapse into touching, kissing, and embracing patients out of a frustrated longing for love.

Pastor Bob sought pastoral counseling after he was reprimanded and told to seek counseling by the church council of a liberal Protestant suburban congregation. At first, he reported that many of the congregants objected to his embracing people at the door. Eventually, however, he admitted that the major issue was a charge of undue familiarity with one of the teenage girls in the youth fellowship. He was shocked and mortified by this allegation, insisting that he felt "absolutely no sexual interest in this young woman." During the course of his counseling, we learned more about the nature of his motivation. He embraced people at the door with an almost evangelical fervor, as though he were saying, "The love we share as fellow Christians must be manifest." Some of the congregants seemed to enjoy the warmth, but it made others squirm. They wouldn't have minded a quick hug, but he made such a production out of it. Perhaps he was going too far to hug the kids in the youth fellowship and to encourage them to hug one another. This one girl felt that his hugging of her went beyond friendliness. He went out of his way to embrace her and his embraces felt too much to her.

The first few counseling sessions were taken up by his feeling totally misunderstood and unappreciated. He went on about how people are too rigid and uptight; how he couldn't understand why the church council was so unsympathetic and unsupportive. He would repeatedly say, "There's nothing wrong with human warmth!" Being put on probation was a devastating blow. He felt all the church council cared about was catering to public opinion, even when it was very narrow-minded.

In the counseling it developed that his mother was never very affectionate or demonstrative. He didn't ever remember being hugged or kissed by her. Nor was she very appreciative of his successes. And so he became a high achiever, striving for really big success, so maybe then people would take notice. It became clear how it was important for him to be powerful and central in the church. He had been to an encounter group workshop, as a part of a retreat, and it was very moving. He got into feelings and into hugging. He brought this with him to the new parish. He didn't sense his congregants' discomfort, because he acted with a kind of zeal and was blind to the undercurrent of sexual tension in his behavior. His grandiose self—that is, the self that blissfully experiences itself normally as the powerful center of all existence—was being maintained through the experience of archaic selfobjects. They are characterized as archaic because the self-support requires physical contact, the literal, tangible presence of another analogous to when the infant requires the mother's touch, the contact-comfort, as a necessary (for survival) selfobject experience. His so-called loving behavior was rationalized as Christian nurture. His powerful need to be held (physically, emotionally, and spiritually) in esteem resulted in his not being aware of the needs of his parishioners and in particular the adolescent female who interpreted his embrace as inappropriate and sexual. He was using them for his own needs, as opposed to theirs, leading to much pain.

To recapitulate, any experience that functions to bring about a cohesive, harmonious, vital sense of self or that maintains the continuity of selfhood is designated as a selfobject experience. In doing psychotherapy, this often means that the patient fulfills a selfobject function for the therapist, such as the therapist's basic need for appreciation. The client serves as a vehicle for meeting previously unmet needs in the psychotherapist. For example, the active smiling and nodding of members in the congregation will bolster the preacher's self-esteem and even reinforce more animated, effective preaching. The preacher's experience of his or her congregation is self-sustaining.

This is also what happens in sports when a team has a come-from-behind rally. Everyone watching has a sense of accomplishment and common purpose. There is a contagious feeling of being connected in an enterprise of overcoming. Imagine how much more powerful is the feeling of sharing in that spirit of communal invigoration when you are the one responsible, the rallying athlete or the professional leader. Successful experience is contagious.

Peggy, a mental health nurse from a general hospital psychiatric unit, entered psychotherapy after making a potentially serious medication error. She complained of malaise and low-grade depression. When she spoke of her sadness, she began to think of all that was missing in her life, "sadly it seems all I ever do is for other people." When she did start to think about the things that made her happy, she had to look back. She remembered the feeling of release she felt each summer when school let out, and she remembered the feeling of ease and freedom she got from swimming in the flooded stone quarry near where she grew up. But her most peaceful and happy memories were of playing the piano. During psychotherapy she resumed her early childhood interest playing the piano. A few months later, for reasons that were not immediately clear, she took up the violin. After several private lessons, she discovered a passion for the violin. "Making music this way is more immediate and direct. It gives me more of a feeling of vitality and inner harmony." She noted that she could see and touch the strings and that it was all up close to her, whereas with the piano the process went from fingers to keys to the invisible piano strings.

During her psychotherapy, we explored the meaning and function of music and why this was being pursued so passionately. She recalled that when she was a child that her singing and humming often served to cheer up her mother. She was thought of as a cheerful, energetic child by her extended family. After more uncovering, Peggy realized that her music-making was expressing a deep-seated longing to comfort and heal a depressed withdrawn mother. Behind the childhood behavior and performances (she called them recitals) she saw a little girl crying out, "What about me?" The price of trying to soothe her mother (provide a selfobject experience for her mother) was the arrested development of her own core sense of self. It now seemed that the violin provided a more effective selfobject experience for her than the piano, perhaps because the piano was for her mother and now the violin was especially for her. As she resumed piano playing her depression lifted; then, the new interest in the violin helped her develop a cohesive, vital, and truly harmonious sense of self. As she became more energized, she regained confidence about her performance at work.

HEALTHY REWARDS IN THE PRACTICE OF PSYCHOTHERAPY

Psychotherapy can be an occasion for therapist selfobject experience, without being exploitative of the patient. It is possible to receive healthy gratification while doing good work.

What would impel a person to spend the bulk of his or her working day immersed in the inner life of another person? Charles Kligerman suggests:

> . . . a need in the analyst to affirm his own self through vicarious mirroring; that is, there is a certain vulnerability of cohesion in a relatively intact self, so that constant repetition creates a rhythmic reaffirmation of the analyst's self while giving functional pleasure in helping another person move toward self-recognition and self-cohesion. Often this resembles the experience of an artist or writer who feels whole or integrated when practicing his art but restless and uneasy when not at work. (1989, p. 258)

Rather than viewing psychotherapy as depleting work, we can see it as deeply sustaining and as itself a source of strength, like a smoothly running operation that does not intrude upon or exploit the patient. Optimally, it is less a question of "physician, heal thyself," than, to quote the poet Gerard Manley

Hopkins (1948), "this seeing the sick endears them to us, us too it endears."

What are some of the satisfactions for the psychotherapist doing psychotherapy and to what extent are they legitimate? Thomas Szasz (1956) elaborated eight types of satisfaction, building on four categories suggested by Ella Sharpe. Her four factors were:

1. Pleasure derived from listening to the unclear complaints of patients because of our ability to interpret and thus make sense out of what is at first confusing. Many of us have been motivated to take up this work because of our desire to figure things out, to "make sense," and to find answers. Psychotherapy seems to be fertile ground for this type of interest and motivation. The danger, of course, is the temptation to impose premature closure or misapply favorite theories. We should remember Bion's (1967) admonition to practice without memory or desire. We believe that those psychotherapists who require high degrees of certainty and are unable to tolerate ambiguity will be at higher risk for burnout. Nevertheless, helping patients organize their experience in meaningful ways usually seems to be a legitimate therapist satisfaction.
2. Satisfactions obtained from achieving mastery over one's own anxieties while working through patient conflicts similar to one's own. This is no doubt a personal benefit and byproduct of doing therapy, a vicarious way of helping ourselves. Obviously, this form of gratification has the potential to compromise or jeopardize treatment. Therapy is most endangered when this variable is unacknowledged. If therapists enter the field in order to solve personal problems, they will often fail their patients and themselves because of the confusion over who needs help. Nevertheless, doing psychotherapy allows us to examine and evaluate ourselves as part of our job and provides occasions for personal growth and development.

3. Satisfaction of a sense of curiosity. Each therapy is an adventure, a chance to make a discovery (in contrast to an opportunity for application of acquired knowledge). The danger in this attitude is becoming too invasive and intrusive. The experience of novelty needs to be balanced with respect for privacy and overexposure. This form of satisfaction, unchecked, could lead to undue familiarity and signal a lack of intimacy in one's personal life.
4. The experience of a rich variety of living through one's contact with many diverse personalities. Psychotherapy is often stimulating work because of the astonishment, amazement, and awe we experience in getting to know other humans. It provides an occasion for broadening our own horizons. A danger exists if we fail to do the objective, detached work of diagnosis and treatment planning. If we become overidentified with our patients and lose sight of the main purpose of our task, we can become ineffective and ultimately burn out.

In addition to these four satisfactions, Thomas Szasz proposes:

5. The pleasure derived from doing "useful work." Following Hendrick,

   > The work principle has been formulated as the need of human beings for the pleasure afforded by the effective integration of the neuromuscular and intellectual functions. It has been emphasized that although generally experienced together with libidinal pleasure, work pleasure is not primarily, displaced or sublimated sensual pleasure. (1943, p. 327)

   There is satisfaction from a job well done. This seems to be largely a legitimate pleasure, although one has to be careful about how "useful" gets defined. Also, burnout is inevitable if one gets *all* one's pleasure from work.
6. The pleasure derived from being needed. Though the

"need to be needed" is related to notions of doing useful work, it probably derives its force from anxieties and doubts connected with the question of "What is the purpose of life?" We answer this question both by procreating and by "creating" in our daily work (e.g., "helping" others, research, the creative arts, watching living things grow, etc.). Although this is a major source of satisfaction, it can become a drawback and source of disappointment when treatment fails. Are we still good therapists when we let go of needing patients to change, so we can concentrate on being understanding and making occasional interpretations? The need to do our job has to remain more important than the need to be needed or liked. Being-there-for-others, however, remains an important motivation, commitment, and source of personal fulfillment for many mental health professionals.

7. Pleasure derived from the mastery of conflicts in human relationships through verbalization and mutual understanding. This may be the most unique aspect of our work. The therapist becomes an active partner in a relationship characterized by emotional upheavals and "misunderstandings" of various kinds, interpersonal stress and disharmony, and then resolution of these situations by thinking and talking rather than persuasion or force. The gratification derives from the pleasure of the successful accomplishment of bits of self-analytic work or working through in the therapist. This is often difficult work; the therapist must be able to tolerate and absorb much painful affect and at the same time remain composed and able to bring to bear his or her best intellectual and emotional resources on the very upheavals taking place. Nevertheless, the satisfactions can be great and serve as a basis for feeling sustained, vigorous, and vital in our work.
8. Pleasure derived from contact with the patient as a protection from loneliness. This may be undesirable; how-

ever, there is pleasure in nonspecific human contact. The therapist's particular personality and actual life situation will largely determine the importance of this factor as a source of gratification.

These satisfactions of the therapist may, under favorable circumstances, lead to the "satisfying" development of the patient as well. For the optimally unhindered psychological development of the patient, acknowledgment of the therapist's psychological satisfactions in his work is desirable. Denial of the therapist's satisfactions in psychotherapy presents the patient with a false picture of the actual interaction and thus interferes with his or her reality-testing. Moreover, in the absence of an honest give-and-take, there is no safeguard against the patient's experiencing in the relationship with the therapist a human interaction similar to that between a child and a masochistic, "self-sacrificing" parent. The burdens and inhibitions which such a relationship can place on the child's emerging sense of self are already familiar to us.

GRANDIOSITY AND THE GOD COMPLEX

Jung's description of the God complex may well describe many psychotherapists. He stated:

> Each profession carries its respective difficulties, and the danger of analysis is that of becoming infected with transference projections. . . . When the patient assumes that his analyst is the fulfillment of his dreams, that he is not an ordinary doctor but a spiritual hero, and a sort of savior . . . he begins to feel if there are saviors, well, perhaps it is just possible I am one. (Jung, 1968, p. 83)

Many patients relate to their therapist as though she were a parent figure, regardless of the therapist's attributes. Idealization of the therapist includes both transference admiration and the operation of a reality factor. The therapist, in a real sense, is an important person to her patients. They come to her in need and she tries to help them. Therapists' experience of patients' depending on them for their well-being and even basic functioning rests upon a grain of truth, which adds to the danger of occupational arrogance. Marmor has said that the hazard will be greater for those therapists who utilize an authoritarian, directive approach than for those using a nondirective one (1953, p. 371).

Because psychotherapy is so personal and intimate, most practices are very "private." The solo practitioner, for example, without supervision or opportunities for sharing clinical work in case conferences, may tend to overestimate the virtue of his own particular approach and ability in contrast to those of his colleagues. A scenario may develop as follows: Over time, it may become more and more evident to her that she really is a sort of extraordinary individual. She may then begin to act touchy and even make herself a nuisance at professional meetings. She becomes disagreeable or withdraws more and more. It then dawns on her that she is really a very important person and of great importance to the profession, the community and beyond. This may lead to unprofessional or unethical conduct. "Pride goeth before destruction and a haughty spirit before a fall," said Solomon.

Remember the awkwardness the psychology intern, Mark, felt when Valerie, the administrative assistant and pastor's wife, complimented him on his "extraordinary warmth and sensitivity." Even more disarming was her statement that she could see herself dating him had they met under different circumstances. This example illustrated the activation of therapist grandiosity and the attempts to defend against it. Idealizing transferences develop where the therapist is seen as the perfect man or woman, lover, or parent. Even though most therapists know intellectually they are not infallible and perfect, idealizations can be so flattering that the therapist may work in certain ways to increase the idealization or to thwart or stifle it altogether. Idealizing transferences collude with the grandiose self. This can begin a vicious feedback loop. The more the therapist attempts to fulfill or gratify the ideal expectations of the patient (thereby using the patient as a mirroring selfobject), the more the patient comes to expect. As a result, the therapist must work even harder to keep up with the expectations so as to preserve the grandiose self.

Some therapists come to believe they have great spiritual significance. About these, Maeder says, "The zealot can find a moral excuse for oppressing others that is unavailable to the mere bully or the charlatan" (1989, p. 44). Deviations from professional standards and alienation within the ranks of the profession may ultimately lead to departure from the profession itself.

Public attitudes are also significant in fostering "God-like" feelings in the psychotherapist. We are all familiar with references to psychiatry and other mental health professions as secular priesthoods and the therapist's office as a new setting for the confessional. Many patients state, "I realize you know what's wrong with me, but you're just trying to get me to figure it out for myself." In social situations, the therapist is often endowed with omniscient qualities ("I'd better watch what I say or you'll read my mind" in response to an introduction) or asked to interpret a dream or explain a behavior problem.

The God Complex in Clergy

The idea for this book originated from our work with clergy (Olsen & Grosch, 1991). If Jung is correct about the God complex as a danger for psychoanalysts, then how much more is it a danger for clergy, who speak on some level for God and are "called" to their vocation?

Clergy frequently feel that they must not only please everyone in the congregation but also satisfy the high expectations of God. If they had parents who were difficult to satisfy, they may feel that it is equally difficult to satisfy God, which adds to the pressure they feel. At the same time, the very difficulty of doing God's work adds to the sense of grandiosity.

If the pastor struggles with accepting his or her own limitations and is overly invested in the grandiose self, which is reinforced by the "God complex," then the situation is further exacerbated by "congregational transference." Transference is described in psychoanalytic theory as the way in which primitive feelings towards parents and significant others are projected onto the analyst. One way this occurs in psychotherapy is that the patient overidealizes the therapist. As therapy progresses and the therapist handles his or her own countertransference reaction to the idealization, this is worked through and the patient withdraws some of the idealization. In a similar way, an idealizing transference occurs in congregational life when a pastor functions as an idealized selfobject with whom parishioners can merge as an image of calmness, infallibility, and perfection. He or she is sought after for advice and spiritual counsel, utilized in times of joy and crisis, and expected on Sundays to deliver a word from God. While intellectually the pastor may know that he/she is being overidealized, it is so flattering that he or she works even harder to keep it coming. Sermons are measured by the number of complimentary comments at the door, and late-night emergency visits are made worthwhile by flattering comments such as, "We could never have come through this crisis without your help." Thus, congregational transference and idealization collude with the pastor's grandiose self. This begins a vicious feedback loop. The more the pastor attempts to be all that the congregation expects him or her to be (thereby using the congregation as a selfobject), the more the congregation expects. One late-night emergency visit leads to more and more late-night visits, until members of the congregation come to expect this type of pastoral service. As a result, the pastor must work even harder to keep up with their expectations and bolster the grandiose self.

Grandiosity, Superiority, and Arrogance

A defensive attitude of arrogance may develop in the therapist with feelings of inadequacy. There are factors inherent in the practice of psychotherapy itself that contribute to this even in the most competent and well-trained therapist. Practicing psychotherapy is infinitely complicated, frequently confusing, and often distressing to the therapist. Therapists feel responsible for alleviating human suffering and misery, preventing suicide and other varieties of dangerousness. Marmor cites "the lack of fixed standards, the necessity of adapting to constantly changing and shifting problems, the complexity of the material, the realistic difficulties involved in achieving success, the constant need to make corrections for subjective blind spots" (1953, p. 372) as sources of anxiety that may encourage a defensive tendency to bolster threatened self-esteem by taking refuge in the God complex.

Undoubtedly you know therapist colleagues who manifest characteristics of this syndrome as originally formulated by Ernest Jones:

> These first manifestations [of the God complex] like those through the whole complex, are most typically reaction-products. Thus obvious self-conceit or vanity is not so frequent or characteristic as an excessive self-modesty, which at times is so pronounced as to be truly a self-effacement. . . . [There is] a tendency to aloofness. [The man] makes himself as inaccessible as possible, and surrounds his personality with a cloud of mystery. One of the most distressing character traits is the attitude of disinclination towards the acceptance of new knowledge. This follows quite logically from the idea of omniscience, for anyone who already knows everything naturally cannot be taught anything new; still less can he admit that he has ever made a mistake in his knowledge. . . . The resentment with which these men observe the growing prominence of younger rivals forms a curious contrast to another character trait, namely, their desire to protect. They are fond of helping, of acting as patron or guardian, and so on. All this, however, happens only under the strict

> condition that the person to be protected acknowledges his helpless position and appeals to them as the weak to the strong. (1951, p. 244)

Consider the example of the clinical psychologist who "surrounds his personality with a cloud of mystery": Dr. K. practices psychotherapy in a suburban New England community. He has a dimly lit waiting room decorated with symbols and artifacts of Eastern religions. There is soft, New Age background music and no secretary. His office or inner sanctum is plushly furnished with a black leather sofa and matching chairs, expensive wall tapestries and exotic carpets. His personal appearance is guru-like; he wears a dashiki shirt and mandala medallion. He routinely begins sessions with portentous silence.

Dr. K.'s decor and appearance are revealing; one message being communicated may be, "We live in different worlds." Maintaining an air of mystery may be a defense against his own anxiety in relation to patients. We believe it is important to look constantly within ourselves to check whether or not the retreat behind a cloak of mystery is a defense against anxiety, a fear of being unable to deal with an emotional relationship with a patient, or perhaps a manifestation of an unconscious attitude of superiority.

Mysteriousness also tends to intensify the idealization of the therapist (Dr. K. is surrounded by images of gods). The less he is viewed as an ordinary human being, the greater the tendency to assume that he is, indeed, perfect and very wise. Many patients will assume that he is a superior psychotherapist because he appears to have knowledge of the world's religions. The atmosphere and conduct of Dr. K.'s practice probably heighten the idealizing aspects of the transference and foster an unconsciously authoritarian parent-child relationship.

Occasionally the feeling of superiority is manifested by the therapist communicating an excessive amount of information about himself or herself. This can be destructive to treatment. Such a therapist is often unconsciously implying, "Be like me." Even though patients often experience temporary relief from their symptoms by imitating a role model, they rarely achieve the kind of enduring benefit that results from discovering and following their own path. Transference improvement, often based on pleasing the therapist, is usually temporary, since it does not coincide with real character change or growth.

In a similar way the psychotherapy supervisor is often motivated by an inner need to demonstrate superior knowledge or experience, since the sense of usefulness as a supervisor is largely dependent on the ability to point out errors of omission or commission to the student. Thus, the supervising therapist has a double occupational hazard. Not only is he exposed to the idealization of his patients, but he also receives deferential treatment from colleagues who are themselves usually extremely competent and intelligent people.

We are by no means implying that all psychotherapists are narcissistic, suffer from a type of God complex, or become arrogant. Rather, we are saying that, when there has not been sufficient mirroring and empathic attunement as the self developed, there may be a compensatory need to be liked, admired, and appreciated, even grandiose. Given the cultural status and title of being a psychotherapist, this may lead to a type of God complex or arrogance, disposing individuals to burnout in many situations.

Although the idea of a God complex may sound a little extreme, all of us have been tempted to play God to our patients at times, not so much because we are inherently arrogant as because we want to meet our patients' longing for someone special to look up to and lean on. Patients, anxious to find someone worthy of their dependent longings, and therapists, anxious to be powerful and wise, collude to create the illusion of an ideal relationship. No wonder that dependency carries with it so much underlying resentment in both parties.

How can one human being be a godlike everything to another? No human relationship can bear the burden of godhood, and the attempt has to take its toll on both parties. When we look for the perfect human object, we are looking for someone who allows us to express our will completely without any frustration or disappointment. We want an object to reflect a truly ideal image of ourselves. God's greatness and power offer nourishment but we must have faith. Meanwhile, wouldn't it be wonderful to find a flesh-and-blood human being as a stand-in? Maybe a therapist.

Then there are the temptations and burdens on the other side of the equation. It's flattering to be admired. It reassures the anxious, insecure part of us that secretly doubts that we know what we're doing. Even if we somehow suspect that we don't really deserve to be so admired, we tell ourselves that the patients need to look up to us. So, if we act a little grand, it's for them. The burden this places on us can weigh us down. We have to be perfect, can't take time off, have to always be there for them, and can't make any mistakes. Then the inevitable disillusion and anger set in, possibly ending in burnout.

Dealing with people's tendency to idealize us leads to two kinds of mistakes. Either we assume that they're right and go along with it, gratifying their ideal expectations, or we are made so anxious by this need that we do everything to deny it, telling them we're just folks, acting like a pal, disclaiming our power, etc. The latter position may be honest, but it denies the role that comes with the territory; after all, patients pay us for having some special expertise. It is a wonder that we ever strike a good enough balance in any sustained fashion.

3

STRAINS IN THE HELPING SYSTEM

Thinking only in terms of individuals without understanding the context in which they live and work will never provide an adequate picture of human experience. Thus, even though self psychology provides a helpful lens for viewing the grand aspirations, and frustrations of many mental health professionals, as well as explaining a propensity towards burnout, it would be reductionistic to imply that burnout is simply the result of narcissistic frustrations. That would leave too many questions unanswered. Consider the following.

George and Michael are both psychologists working as clinical directors in mental health centers. Both have a strong desire to be admired and admit to craving attention from those around them. George, however, likes his work, considers himself successful, and is generally pleased with the progress of his professional career. He also enjoys the time he spends outside of work with his friends and with his family. Michael, on the other hand, feels disillusioned, tired, and discouraged. He frequently daydreams about being in another profession. He wonders if he could learn to work with computers and fantasizes about becoming a much-sought-after consultant.

How are we to understand the differences between these two people? Why is one struggling with burnout and depression, questioning his career choice, while the other is happy and satisfied? Simply utilizing the insights of self psychology, or any individually oriented psychology for that matter, to understand their personalities won't suffice. People don't live or work in a vacuum; they operate in a complex variety of systems that affect the way they see themselves and their world.

The tendency to view our lives on this planet from the solipsistic perspective of individualism obscures the larger view that we are a part of systems within systems: the family, the extended family, the office, the caregiving system, the community—vast networks of association. We think of ourselves as individuals and hope to be heroes, but we are embedded in networks that define and sustain us. We often feel significantly determined, if not fated, by what happened to us in childhood. But Freud left us the hope that with self-understanding and insight, a better adaptation, if not happiness, will be assured. The truth is that looking inside ourselves can show us only part of the interpersonal world of our human nature and part of the reason for our feeling incomplete and dissatisfied.

Freud's theories were taken as encouragement to overcome guilty fear in favor of self-expression and freedom. Other people, in this framework, were objects of our desire. Michael's imagined solution to his malaise of leaving his unfulfilling relationships at work and finding another situation is thoroughly consistent with this psychological perspective. Nevertheless, burnout is best explained by examining not simply individual variables or environmental contexts and pressures, but the interaction of self and environment. General systems theory is helpful in providing the bridge between the two.

SYSTEMS THEORY DEFINED

Although systems theory has become identified with family therapy, general systems theory is a whole new way of seeing and thinking rather than just a particular set of family therapy techniques. Systems theory is concerned with understanding the relationship of the whole with its interacting parts, and the interaction of both with the larger environment (von Bertalanffy, 1968). When applied to families, systems theory looks at the individual in the context of that person's family and the family as part of the larger culture. As a theory, it is concerned with how systems regulate themselves so that homeostasis is preserved. As a result, systems theory insists on understanding people in the context of the environment in which they live, rather than solely in intrapsychic terms.

Family systems theory owes much of its inspiration to the late Gregory Bateson (1972) and his group of researchers in Palo Alto, California. Bateson's theories became a springboard for the application of systems theory to family therapy and for understanding human behavior from an interactional perspective. While the family therapy field has moved in many different directions during the course of its development, several important and familiar systems constructs are helpful in understanding the problem of burnout.

One obvious feature of family systems theory is a shift in emphasis from the personal to the interpersonal. Systems theory focuses on the family's role in the development of problems and how current relationships (family and other) maintain and exacerbate these problems. It seeks to understand persons in the context of the systems in which they live and work and to uncover the impact of those systems upon the self. Thus, in terms of burnout, systems theorists would look for the ways in which the mental health professional interacts with the work system, and the interactional effect that can result, as individuals deal with issues such as rigid beauracratic structures, poor clinical supervision, funding cutbacks, and expanding caseloads.

The concept of circular causality is helpful in amplifying this picture.

Since everyone in a system is interrelated, a change in any one member affects other individuals and the group as a whole. The first person is then affected by the changes in the others in a circular chain of influence. Causality is seen as circular not linear, as in older psychoanalytic models, in which etiology was conceived in terms of prior events that produced symptoms in the present. For example, in any institution employees are part of an interrelated system. Change anywhere in the organization will have an impact on the entire system. Thus, if there are budget cutbacks and secretarial staff is reduced, the entire agency is stressed. In much the same way, if a supervisor assumes a patronizing attitude and insists that his or her supervisees practice according to the supervisor's personal therapeutic paradigm, there will be a ripple effect throughout the agency. Triangles will be formed as therapists form alliances against the "bad supervisor" and unofficially designate another supervisor as the good supervisor. This may lead to squabbling, tension, and a generally poisoned atmosphere. Coffee breaks begin to center around discussions on how unfair the supervisor, director, or boss is. Obviously, if people are preoccupied with resentment and blaming the boss, they'll have less energy and interest in doing their work.

Everywhere around us we're encouraged to think of our own needs. When we're feeling beleaguered and insecure, it's natural to think about looking out for number one, rather than thinking about our connection to others. In this frame of mind, linear thinking encourages us to think of ourselves as victims of other people and circumstances. The alternative is not only circular—we're all in this together—but also empowering—by looking at the way we influence and are influenced in turn by others, we can begin to change the systems of which we are a part.

Finally, systems theory, as has already been implied, stresses circularity in communication. Behavior as well as communication is frequently governed by feedback loops. For example, if a wife takes responsibility for everything, her husband may take responsibility for nothing. The less he does the more she does, and the more she does the less he does. The interaction is complementary and mutually reinforcing, trapping both husband and wife in rigid and polarized roles. Other examples of mutual influence are an assertive wife and a submissive husband, or a pursuing wife and a distancing husband. Up close, the partners themselves may only feel their hurt and see the other one's maddening role in "causing" it. Seen from a distance, however, they are partners in a circular—and very painful—process. Their polarized interactions are perpetuated by complementary feedback loops. Stepping back to see what's going on—that's the hard part.

MURRAY BOWEN AND NATURAL SYSTEMS THEORY

Utilizing systems theory and ideas about complementary feedback loops does not mean that we must ignore the legacy of the past. Bowen's theory (1978; Kerr & Bowen, 1988) is an invaluable resource in expanding the concept of feedback loops by adding a multigenerational perspective. A central notion of Bowenian theory is *differentiation of self*. Bowen suggests that people deal with their families of origin with a wide range of responses, along a continuum from cut-off on one extreme to fusion on the other. Those who cut off from their families of origin deal with the anxiety of their family systems as well as family games and triangles by moving away physically and/or emotionally and staying distant from the family. Those who remain fused with their families cannot think or act independently.

Ironically, Bowen's theory holds that persons on either extreme have failed to differentiate from their family of origin. They are unable to hold objective distance, what Edwin Friedman calls non-anxious presence (1985, p. 208), from their families of origin, and as a result they may often be in a reactive mode. Both those who are cut-off and those who are fused are still tied emotionally to their families. As a result, triangles from their families of origin tend to be replicated in other contemporary relationships.

The work environment has an uncanny way of becoming a second family, in which one frequently plays the same role one played in one's family of origin. Frequently, mental health professionals find themselves playing the same roles in present work relationships that they were trapped in as children. For example, if a child's parents cannot resolve their marital conflicts, the child is frequently triangulated in an unhealthy relationship with one of the parents, as the child plays the role of confidant, or marital counselor, or substitute spouse. The child winds up feeling responsible for that parent. This triangle will likely be replayed over and over again in the present. As a working adult, the therapist who sided with one parent against the other may encourage the secretary to complain about the boss, sow dissension through gossip, side with patients against clinic policy, or take sides in patient families. Thus we were not surprised when talking with a social worker on the verge of burnout to discover that he had been his mother's protector and pseudo-husband, defending her and his siblings from an abusive father. Now he had become an advocate for the downtrodden, overinvolved and overresponsible with his clients, and oversolicitous with fellow staff members who came to him for advice. The point isn't that there's something wrong with being helpful. The point is that this social worker had learned to protect others in a way that kept them from taking care of themselves. Their helplessness made him feel powerful. As a result, he became too busy rescuing other people to take care of his own work responsibilities and outside relationships.

Utilizing the systems theory notion of feedback loops in concert with Bowen's multigenerational theory, we see an added dimension of burnout. One's role in the family of origin, as well as one's level of differentiation of self, will have an impact on the way one functions at work. Despite what we know about how we are supposed to function, when we get anxious we often abandon that rational perspective (or react like any creature who's frightened: panicky). For example, many of us flee confrontations at work and avoid saying hard things to people because we learned growing up to avoid conflict at all costs. Dan, who works as the executive director of a family counseling center, is one such person. He has avoided facing two of his staff members about their chronic lateness and oppositional attitudes in staff meetings. He's afraid that facing them will result in an angry blow-up. As a result, he comes to work anxious to avoid conflict but aware of all the triangles that are emerging as other staff members talk about what is going on and resent his lack of decisive leadership. The family counseling center has become a dysfunctional system, unwittingly replicating the unhealthy structure of many of the families it is trying to help.

Hundreds of examples could be given of professionals who put in long hours not simply to get the job done but to make sure they are liked and admired by coworkers, or of those who overfunction to compensate for those who underfunction around them, suffering in silence, agents of their own misfortune. There are those who exhaust themselves emotionally at the office, not simply dealing with client needs but staying finely tuned to the emotional needs of everyone around them, as if they had built-in radar. Bowen theory helps explain why the workplace brings out in professionals roles similar to those they played in their families. If they have been involved in dysfunctional feedback loops in their family of origin, then these replays at work are particularly toxic.

THE THERAPIST'S SYSTEMS: A WIDE VARIETY OF FEEDBACK LOOPS

As one realizes the power of various feedback loops, the influence of our family of origin as well as current family, and the role we play in a great number of systems (family, work team, friends, and professional organizations), the interplay of person and system becomes easier to understand. We never function in a vacuum.

Human behavior and personality are embedded in a variety of contexts, each of which exerts pressure and makes demands (see Figure 1). For example, a professional who is already predisposed to overfunction may find herself in the position of trying to accommodate a greater client caseload to cut down waiting lists, dealing with her husband's and children's expectations for more of her time at home, and at the same time trying to meet committee expectations of a professional organization. The accumulation of stresses gives the word "pressure" new meaning!

Mental health professionals need to be aware of the various systems and contexts in which they operate; yet, poor differentiation of self makes it difficult to see the trap in which one is caught, much less to remain appropriately defined in those contexts. In times of stress and anxiety we revert to older, less mature ways of relating, learned in our families of origin. As a result we run like hamsters around the feedback loop. For example, most of us know that it is important not to pursue a distancer. Yet in times of anxiety we easily forget that lesson

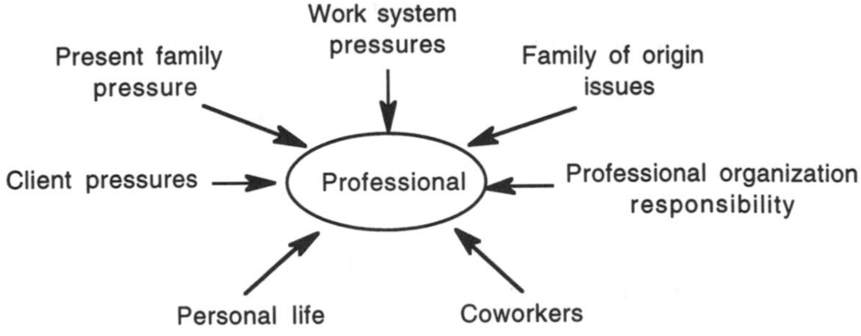

Figure 1: The Multisystem Pressures on the Professional

and pursue with great energy, which of course results in more distance and frustration all around.

Joann is a supervisor in a community mental health clinic. She knows that, whenever she pursues certain staff members who are chronically behind in their case reports, they come up with ever more elaborate excuses. And the more she presses, the more stubbornly they resist. As a result, the agency becomes further backed up on paperwork, and Joann, in an attempt to be understanding, lets the behavior continue. She knows that pursuing in this manner gets her nowhere. She also knows that she needs to take a hard line with clear penalties, but she can't bring herself to crack down. She doesn't want to be thought of as authoritarian, which was the way she viewed her father. As a result, she winds up working longer and longer hours to compensate for the staff members she has been pursuing. She becomes distant and overresponsible in a way that allows others to be underresponsible. How often do professionals put in longer and longer hours, like Joann, to compensate for the underresponsible behavior of those around them?

Notice that Joann's self-defeating pattern isn't simple. She doesn't just nag, she also backs off when her staff gets resentful. So her problem maintaining behavior is a combination of nagging and backing off. That's often the way with our contributions to our own dilemmas—and that's why our errors aren't always easy for us to see.

In order to understand and prevent burnout, we need to consider the possible destructive loops in our own work settings. As we look at our difficulties in defining our position in the midst of these loops we will gain a more sophisticated view of our risk of becoming overloaded, if not overwhelmed.

Problematic feedback loops are complicated by two additional factors: gender and the dual-career marriage. Himle, Jayaratne, and Chess (1987) found that decreased emotional support from supervisors and coworkers correlates with emotional exhaustion and irritation in women, but not in men. This suggests that, in dealing with the pressures of work that lead to burnout, good supervision and peer support are more important for women than for men.

The multiplicity of roles in which women professionals find themselves can make balancing roles more difficult than for men. While historically men have been free to define themselves and create meaning through their work, for women the issue is not as simple. Many female professionals have a difficult time not feeling the total responsibility for the maintenance and emotional well-being of the family. Frequently, role-sharing by professionals in a marriage leaves much to be desired. Too often, even professional women find themselves stressed by the reality that they are expected to be in charge of everything at home while experiencing tremendous demands at work.

Finally, women professionals unfortunately have to deal with sex discrimination and sexual harassment on the job, which further exacerbates stress. The same woman who isn't taken seriously by her male counterparts may have to fend off unwanted personal attention while seeking professional recognition and validation. This leaves the female professionals in a bind. Does she wear the stylish dresses she likes, or does that make her appear too "feminine" and not "serious"? Does she smile and act friendly, or does that seem flirtatious? Does she develop a tough, businesslike edge, or does that make her seem hard and mean? Does she concentrate on developing relationships with other women at work, or does that shut her out of the power loop?

Professionals in dual-career marriages may experience increased stress from balancing multiple roles. In dual-career marriages it is all too easy to get into symmetrical feedback loops, where no one backs down, around difficult questions: Whose career takes precedence? Who stays home to care for sick kids? What happens when one gets a transfer? Delicate balance and negotiation are required, squeezing the therapist who feels he or she "already gave at the office."

The Therapist-Client Feedback Loop

The most obvious feedback loop in which the therapist participates is the therapist-client system. Traditionally, the interaction between therapist and client has been described in terms of transference and countertransference. Transference is understood as the feelings that are transferred by the patient from earlier relationships, usually parental, to the therapist. Thus the therapist may be seen as father, mother, lover, friend, or rival. Transference includes a wide range of other feelings, including idealization: "You are the most brilliant person I have ever met. You always understand me." A "mirroring transference" forms when the client needs to be seen in a particular way by the therapist. Countertransference refers to the feelings triggered in the therapist by the client.

Most professionals have been trained to think in these terms; sometimes, however, the technical terms serve to distance us from the real feelings that get stirred up in the therapeutic process. It's one thing to describe these emotions as "transference," quite another to deal with very attractive or influential clients who idealize you and consistently tell you that you are the most understanding and brilliant therapist they have ever encountered and that they wish they hadn't wasted so much time with previous therapists. While professionally we have been trained to understand idealization as a manifestation of transference, at times it feels so good that we begin to believe it. Who doesn't occasionally believe that he or she is unusually gifted?

Susceptibility to idealization becomes a particularly powerful dynamic if within the therapist's family of origin there was inadequate mirroring or parental responsiveness, or if the therapist is feeling unappreciated at home now. It's all too easy to seek the mirroring he or she craves and did not receive in the family of origin by recreating a work family of clients and staff. As this occurs, a complementary interactional feedback loop is set up in which the therapist colludes with the idealization and begins to work harder to deliver more brilliant interpretations in order to solicit more idealization. So begins a powerful feedback loop. The harder the therapist works, the more idealizing statements are made. The more idealization that is bestowed, the harder the therapist works. It's not just working harder, either; it's draining to always be pleasing, to always need to be admired. So, at the same time more energy is being exerted, less good work may be getting done.

One of our clients, Daren, acknowledged that working in an urban family services center was far from easy, and added that even his frayed office was depressing. As he attempted to make changes in families carrying multigenerational legacies of abuse, alcoholism, and poverty, he often felt totally ineffective, and often hopeless.

Daren spoke wearily about his work; however, when he talked about several individuals and couples he was currently working with, he began to smile. With a little embarrassment he talked about how they frequently told him that working with him was the one bright spot in their lives, and how much they looked forward to their sessions with him. Not surprisingly, Daren also looked forward to his sessions with these clients, both as a relief from some of the other multiproblem families and as a boost to his professional confidence.

The problem was that the feedback from these clients motivated Daren to work even harder to provide help for them. He began to feel that he was the one person who could make a difference in their lives. Forgetting that his clients must ultimately make their own changes, which frequently come in small steps, Daren tried harder and harder to make things happen. As a result he worked longer and longer hours, routinely getting overinvolved with his clients, until he reached the point of exhaustion. Caught unawares in a feedback loop, he felt unable to go on. When one of his favorite clients terminated without ever showing up for the last session, he felt something broke inside. When he came to see us he was having a hard time recovering his vocational enthusiasm, and was in fact on the verge of despair.

Variations on this theme exist in many other professional relationships. For example, the clergyperson who makes a late-night emergency visit to a family in crisis is rewarded with feedback like "Pastor, we would never have made it without your help. You're always there when we need you." This idealization leads to more and more late-night emergency visits, in turn leading to more idealization. The collusion process has locked pastor and parishioner into a complementary feedback loop, which may have as its outcome the burnout of the pastor. In the same manner, the social worker who begins to build a caseload of dependent personalities and enjoys their flattering idealization and adoration gets caught up in a similar feedback loop, leading to working longer hours and ever harder to satisfy the seeming insatiable appetites of her clients.

It is easy to think of these overextended professionals as utilizing bad judgment, easy to objectify and dehumanize their dilemmas by describing them in terms of countertransference. Too often, however, the therapist or mental health professional has played these rescuing roles before, usually in the family of origin. The lessons we learn in our families exert a powerful hold. What's easy to see in others may be hard to see in ourselves—hard to see, harder still to change.

The Helper and Present Family Responsibilities

Too often the systems in which professionals find themselves end up clashing. For example, while mental health professionals are feeding their grandiosity by spending longer and longer hours being as helpful as they can to a wide number of clients, their own families frequently feel shortchanged. After a long day of seeing clients, how many professionals feel like listening to their partners complain about their lack of emotional availability, or the kids demand more help writing the history report that's due tomorrow? How often do mental health professionals hear from their families comments like "Schedule me an appointment and maybe then you'll listen to me!"

Too often, professionals who are empathic all day, and at times into the night, long to come home and collapse in front of the television and not think about anything. Frequently when their partners want to talk, they have no emotional energy left. The same helper who is seen as a hero or sensitive healer by clients is a louse at home.

So much for a complementary feedback loop or for grandiosity being reinforced by family. Hitting reality at home can be an unnerving experience, leading to anger and withdrawal and in turn to more time spent at the office to escape the "ungrateful" and "demanding" family. One person we know who works long hours and is adored by his staff refers to his wife's complaints that he's never around and misses the children's athletic events and school functions as "C.C.E.D."—constant complaining and endless dissatisfaction.

The professional helper has one type of experience at work and a very different one at home. For example, Peter just completed a therapy session with Donna, an attractive professional woman. As they talked, she crossed her legs somewhat carelessly and let her skirt hitch up; Peter could not help but notice. Towards the end of the session, she said to Peter, "This is the only place I really feel safe. It's as if you know what I'm going to say even before I say it." Peter left the office feeling good, since this was his last session for the day. As he entered his home, his wife, who'd had a long day as an administrator for a large nursing home, called from the kitchen that she was tired of his coming home late and assuming she would have dinner ready. "Sometimes I wonder if you ever think of anyone but yourself," she added. Immediately, Peter found himself thinking of what his attractive last client had said, and he withdrew angrily to another room without responding.

Peter had just experienced two different interactions. The first was complimentary and reinforced his grandiosity, while the second left him angry, sullen, and feeling totally unappreciated. The demands of two competing systems are setting up escalating feedback spirals that feed on each other; for the individual this process can feel like a whipsaw.

Other pressures have nothing to do with grandiosity. Who hasn't had the experience of being hopelessly behind at work, buried under mounds of paperwork, without sufficient clerical help, only to realize that it is your night to drive carpool? Such conflicts are a common part of marriage, especially for dual-career couples. Balancing roles, splitting housework, attempting to share childcare responsibilities leave both spouses feeling resentful—*someone* clearly isn't pulling his or her weight. Unfortunately it's all too easy for therapists to forget the conflict-negotiation skills they help other couples develop. It's easier to fantasize about patients or at least about someone who would function better as a "mirroring selfobject" to support their grandiosity—someone who would see them as they would like to be seen without always reminding them of their shortcomings. Who doesn't occasionally resonate with the line in the fairy tale, "Mirror mirror on the wall, who's the fairest of them all?" All too often it's easier to find mirrors that will show us what we want to see outside of the home.

Gender, too, is a factor in who gets overloaded. A man may struggle with his longing for his wife to be a mirror of his grandiosity, too easily forgetting the demands on his wife's energy. As Ambrose Bierce wrote in *The Devil's Dictionary*: "Egoist. A person of low taste, more interested in herself than me." A woman may be wrestling with her anger at balancing all of her responsibilities at work, especially in a helping profession, with feeling responsible at home for the emotional needs of everyone in the family. When there is consistent role inequity, as many women professionals experience, the work environment may actually become a more inviting, apparently manageable environment. At least the day has a beginning and an end. This, of course, sets up a feedback loop leading to overwork.

These feedback loops can be further complicated by family

life-cycle issues. Carter and McGoldrick (1989) describe six stages of the family life cycle: (1) leaving home as single young adults, (2) the joining of families through marriage and formation of the new couple, (3) families with young children, (4) families with adolescents, (5) launching children and moving on, and (6) families in later life. With each of these developmental stages there are predictable crises and developmental tasks that must be mastered for the family to go forward in a healthy way. Obviously, these developmental challenges place great demands on the energy of the professional helper. How similar developmental issues were dealt with in the family of origin may extenuate or exacerbate life-cycle transitions.

Crises and problems can easily become exaggerated during any one of the family life-cycles stages. Consider the family with adolescent children. A number of issues may be coming together, creating a great deal of stress within the family. Adolescents are notorious for challenging family boundaries and values as they attempt to form their own identities. Parents must struggle to remain empathically attuned to these adolescents or young adults, while at the same time maintaining appropriate boundaries. As if that is not enough of a challenge, the marriage itself may be strained by parenting and vocational demands on either or both mother and father. Midlife may be the time of greatest demand vocationally, just when teenagers need more from their parents. Not surprisingly, crises arise, as father or mother or both re-evaluate their life paths and struggle to find meaning. Sailing a boat to a far-away island may sound like an attractive option.

The issue is not always insufficient or inappropriate mirroring at work. The reality is that marital problems and pressures at home also cause work stress. Results of three studies involving 1,187 participants showed that burnout symptoms were more related to marital problems than to work stress (Pines & Aronsen, 1988). This is an important finding considering that too often men in particular concentrate their best energies on their careers in a mistaken belief that their marriages will somehow take care of themselves.

Career and marriage burnout affect each other. When we start stressing out at work, we typically pull back from coworkers and isolate ourselves. We think we aren't getting enough recognition or the work isn't challenging enough, so we make increasing demands on our spouses to entertain and appreciate us. Such demands are unfair and unrealistic to the extent that we're asking our partners to make up for all the missing satisfaction in our lives.

Burnout can work the other way, too, spilling over from marriage to work. Most often this involves people who escape marital problems by immersing themselves in their work. They come to work early, leave late, and take work home to shield themselves from emotional contact with their families. As long as they remain successful, they can usually avoid trouble. But once a work crisis occurs, they have nothing to fall back on at home.

The Professional's Family of Origin

In addition to dealing with both work systems and spouse and children, mental health professionals are involved with their families of origin in ways that are both obvious and not so obvious. The involvement is obvious in the case of the professional who still gets desperate calls from his mother begging him to do something with her alcoholic second husband; these calls leave him feeling helpless and angry, both at his inability to help and at his chronically complaining mother. It is not so obvious in the case of those professionals who believe that they have dealt with their family issues in individual therapy and resolved them by seeing family members as little as possible while claiming the relationships are fine. These individuals consider themselves independent from their families, but they may be acting out the consequences of their emotional cut-off in a number of ways. They may continue to play the same role at work that they played at home, or manifest at work an inability to handle conflict, or feel empty and needy and so expect too much from coworkers or even clients. Without realizing it they are still being influenced by their families and are caught in yet another problematic feedback loop.

Multigenerational theorists (Bowen, 1978; Brown, 1991; E. Friedman, 1985) describe problems as having horizontal and vertical dimensions. Deep struggles within our families of origin and our roles within those families are reenacted across a number of situations in the present. The more dysfunctional one's family of origin, the more unfinished business we have with them (or they leave behind).

Consider the case of Jan, the oldest of five children in an alcoholic family. As the oldest she was the family "hero" and was responsible for everything from parenting her younger siblings to cooking the family meals to being her alcoholic mother's nurse. What kept her going were the accolades she received from her father for being so "mature and unselfish." Her needs were constantly neglected. Not surprisingly, in her capacity as a supervising psychiatric nurse, she found it impossible to say no. She was consistently overresponsible, working much longer hours than her shift required. She had a habit of "rescuing" her patients, leading to frequent criticism from her superior, which she experienced as devastating. Meanwhile, Jan's siblings and mother continued to call her for advice and often for money as well.

Jan's work-related problems and the fact that she was on the road to burnout had horizontal and vertical dimensions. The vertical dimension was Jan's largely unconscious memory of her father's comments, which had a selfobject function of sustaining her grandiosity while at the same time trapping her in a perpetually overresponsible mode. The horizontal level, that of her work environment, replicated her family of origin. The more she functioned in an overresponsible mode, the more those around her underfunctioned, just as her family did. As long as she received positive reviews and much praise from her supervisors, she continued in the same overresponsible mode. This feedback loop, which replicated her family, made appropriate self-definition and boundary-setting all but impossible. However, negative reviews were devastating. Working in an underfunctioning unit while at the same time receiving desperate calls from her family of origin pushed Jan, unable to set boundaries with either "family," closer and closer to burnout.

We repeat patterns in order to replay and reexperience significant relationships and roles as well as to seek experiences that we missed. Attempts (often unconscious) are made to force close relationships to fit the internal role models. Moreover, what we internalize are interactional patterns (more so than discrete images of objects), which we recreate in our present life. It seems that these patterns, once internalized, cannot remain self-contained; they push for expression and reenactment in the external world.

Family of origin demands in the present can also exert powerful pressures on those in the helping professions in a number of ways. One rather annoying pressure is being "therapist" in the family with all the flattery and burden that represents. This may mean being the one the family feels free to call for advice, which is of course rarely followed. Most professionals can relate to coming home after an emotionally exhausting day, only to receive a phone call from a sibling reciting a long list of marital woes, and then asking for some free therapeutic advice. It is difficult to be polite in these situations, especially knowing the advice isn't likely to be taken. These phone calls, or the experiences of being cornered at a family party by a distressed cousin, or visiting one's parents only to hear about their marital tensions, all add increased pressure in the life of the professional.

However, while these pressures are annoying and irritating,

they do not compare to the pressures of dealing with aging parents. As we know all too well, as parents age roles shift and we are frequently called upon to care for them. Doing psychotherapy, working with families, or sitting through administrative board meetings, while at the same time waiting for the phone to ring letting you know that a parent's medical condition is deteriorating rapidly, frequently leaves us feeling anxious, exhausted, helpless, and unable to concentrate.

Charlotte, for example, came for therapy stating that she felt like she was in a trance, simply going through the motions. Her 80-year-old mother was dying of cancer in a nearby hospital, while her father was at home unable to care for himself. Charlotte felt torn between the pressures of her work as a psychologist, calling doctors daily to check on her mother's condition and making difficult medical decisions, the never ending phone calls from her father who was rapidly becoming disoriented by what was happening. Charlotte was beginning to feel like she could no longer function, and was afraid she would "lose it" under the pressure. She acknowledged that all this involvement with her parents was again putting her by necessity in the overresponsible mode, and stirring up old unresolved family of origin issues. Coping with the health-care crises of aging parents, and making decisions about their care may all stir up unresolved family of origin issues just when work pressures may be at a peak. Again the professional is caught between a variety of powerful pressures.

What happens to the professional who is trying to manage work-related stress, deal with aging and sick parents, keep a marriage vital, and raise adolescent children? Where does such an overburdened person find relief? Perhaps by breaking down.

The Helper and Bureaucracy

There is no escaping bureaucracy. Most mental health professionals enter their professions with tremendous enthusiasm and idealism, anxious to make the world a better place by helping people in pain. They don't count on bureaucratic red tape, utilization reviews, chart work, insurance forms, treatment plans and updated treatment plans and telephone reviews for managed care companies, special forms required for HMOs, not to mention inadequate secretarial support to assist in the typing, photocopying and filing. Budget cuts make the problem worse by providing less and less agency support. How often do therapists say angrily, "All I want to do is work with my clients! Why can't someone do the paperwork so I can do what I was trained to do?" Frequently, they find themselves with an ever expanding caseload, long hours of mandated paperwork, poor support services, working in offices that are too small, too noisy, and desperately in need of new furniture. Fantasies of escaping it all to a lucrative private practice fade rapidly in light of declining insurance reimbursement, HMOs, managed care, and recession.

After more than a decade of state and federal cutbacks, these practical pressures are more burdensome than ever. Suzanne, a clinical social worker in a large county mental health clinic, reported that she can no longer deal with the pressures, and wondered aloud why she ever went into social work in the first place. She had entered the field with high ideals, anxious to help families in crisis. Initially she enjoyed her work and felt very good about her work with families. However, after working for seven years in the same agency, with very little clerical support to help with paperwork for an ever increasing caseload of multiproblem families and marginally functioning individuals who "no showed" regularly, she began to experience feelings of burnout. As she wrestled with her decision to leave the profession, she talked repeatedly about the administrative and bureaucratic pressures. Even supervision began to focus on how paperwork and utilization reviews were to be written up and maintained.

Unfortunately, stories like this are not unusual. Regardless of their discipline, many professionals can relate to being caught in escalating bureaucratic feedback loops. Too often helping professionals are evaluated on their administrative, rather than clinical skills. Creativity and clinical excellence are not rewarded either financially or administratively. As a result it is easy to feel constantly criticized and rarely affirmed. Self-esteem is soon smothered under the weight of bureaucracy and negative feedback.

Another variation of this theme involves paradigm clashes, where mental health professionals find that their therapeutic paradigm is at odds with that of the agency. What happens, for example, to the family systems therapist who finds himself/herself working with a supervisor who believes in working only with individuals? Or the therapist who attempts to work psychodynamically within a medical setting? The context in which one works, and the primary paradigm of that context, can enable one to flourish or suffocate one's creativity.

There is a pull toward homeostasis in any system. All the well-intentioned creativity and idealism that young professionals bring to their jobs is rarely sufficient to counteract this pull and change a system. The ultimate irony for many therapists is that they may experience success in helping families change dysfunctional structures and patterns while working within a dysfunctional setting they feel helpless to change. It's hard for them to see their role in perpetuating the status quo, and even harder to influence those in charge. As family therapists know, frequently structure and hierarchies must be changed within families in order for significant change to occur. Within agencies structures and hierarchies are very difficult, if not impossible, to change. Like families, agencies often have a long history of dysfunctional patterns, which are resistant to change. In these contexts, idealism and enthusiasm die a slow death.

The Supervisory Feedback Loop

Supervision can be a blessing or a curse. The quality of supervision may spell the difference between a rewarding career, in which a therapist learns and grows, and a deadening one, in which a therapist flounders for want of useful advice or slowly loses confidence in the face of constant criticism. Good supervision is quite helpful in preventing burnout. It can be affirming and educational when it addresses the supervisee's learning goals and difficult cases. However, as many in the helping professions can attest, supervision is not always helpful. Sometimes it is a negative or even abusive experience. Supervision becomes counterproductive or even destructive when supervisors need to keep those they are supervising in a one-down position by constantly finding something wrong with their work, by ignoring their individuality and humanity, or by imposing a particular paradigm on supervisees. Barbara, for example, reported coming to supervision with a sense of dread. Reviewing videotapes with her supervisor became an opportunity for him to pick apart her work and point out how he would have handled the case much differently and, he implied, much better. The critical tone of his voice would leave Barbara angry and frustrated, but she was afraid to confront him about the quality of the supervision since he had the power to fire her.

In other cases, boundaries between supervision and psychotherapy are ignored and the supervisor begins to practice invasive supervision, attempting to be both supervisor and psychotherapist. Phil talked about how his supervisor constantly asked him about his countertransference reactions to clients, and then used this material as a way to expose Phil's personal problems. When Phil protested, he was labeled resistant to supervisory input.

Frequently, in agencies the context of supervision where supervisors are usually both supervisors and administrators is ignored. In these situations supervision is never really safe, since the supervisor has a powerful voice in job evaluations. Abuses may occur more frequently when female therapists have male supervisors, since the situation replicates gender inequities and power imbalances in our society. These abusive supervisory relationships can become the ultimate negative feedback loop. How does a person fight back against a supervisor who has the power to fire you? The heightened anxiety and grinding discouragement of this situation set the stage for burnout.

The Personal Life of the Therapist

While the mental health professional operates in a wide variety of feedback loops he or she also carries on a personal life (or hopes to anyway). However, mental health professionals may find it difficult to turn off their "analytic side" and relax with friends. On the other side, friends may feel self-conscious and worry that they are being analyzed.

One of the burdens on modern marriage is that diminishing ties to the extended family have not been compensated by expanding friendships. At certain stages of our lives we tend to focus so much energy on our career or one relationship that our lives get out of balance. The more narcissistically vulnerable among us tend to cultivate a radical individualism. It isn't a matter of loving ourselves more than other people; rather, we are too preoccupied with ourselves to have time for others. This may be compounded in a profession where "time is money," so that we set a high valuation on our time. The time required for friendship gets sacrificed when we are focused on success and material goods.

Too often therapists have few friends and delude themselves into thinking that they have such intimate relationships with clients that they do not need friends. How does one move from the discussion of the intimate details of a patient's life, or from the analysis of an existential crisis, to the idle chatter of a cocktail party? However, therapists with few friends become more and more reliant on their clients as sources of self-esteem. This becomes dangerous for both therapist and client.

Some therapists progressively turn some long-term clients into friends. This often begins with self-disclosure on the part of the therapist. While some self-disclosure may be therapeutically useful, many therapists don't know where to draw the line. Slowly they begin to confide too much of their lives to their clients, theoretically to help their clients but most likely because they are lonely. Therapy sessions become mutual sharing times or friendly social hours over coffee. Obviously, this makes for poor therapy. In addition, therapy becomes valuable to the therapist as a social event, encouraging further withdrawal from normal social occasions. Flexibility and balance are lost. Unfortunately, therapists who become one-dimensional in this way are unlikely to be therapeutically flexible and to change on their own.

4

CONTRIBUTIONS TO BURNOUT FROM INNER AND OUTER SPACE

Undoubtedly, there are work situations so stressful and burdensome that they would exhaust the resources of almost anyone. But whether or not burnout occurs depends on the internal state of the person experiencing the lived events and the way in which the person expresses herself in the system. In an interactional approach we assume that neither individual characteristics nor aspects of the environment solely determine burnout. Rather, the way in which the helper defines herself to the system is a product of both personal family development and the current work system. The less cohesive the self, the less self-definition in the work system. When this is combined with a stressful work environment the conditions for burnout are ripe.

Connie never cared much for playing games. She went into mental health work because she wanted to reach out and relate to people on an authentic level; she wanted to get at the heart of human nature. Earlier in her career she loved being someone others confided in, someone who could help. However, by the time she sought professional help because of chronic fatigue and vague feelings of nausea, she woke up each morning with anxiety and dread, feeling as though she could not face one more day of work.

Connie, a 37-year-old single woman, worked as a psychiatric rehabilitation counselor in a residential program for children and adolescents. At the first counseling session, she conveyed a sense of futility and purposelessness and said that nothing she did mattered. Unable to get herself going in the morning and yet afraid of facing criticism from coworkers and the facility director, she frequently arrived late for work. Recently she had made some mistakes because of difficulty concentrating and paying attention in staff meetings. Fearful of losing her job, she recognized that something had to change.

In the second session, Connie described an awkward situation where the mother of her colleague worked at the same residence. When there were problems on their unit, her coworker would run to her mother for advice, and then both would criticize Connie for her efforts and initiatives. Worse yet, her coworker's mother was also the sister of the facility director. Connie was reluctant to go to the director concerning conflicts with this counselor and her mother because she assumed he would side with his sister and niece against her. The threesome often took coffee breaks and meals together, rarely inviting Connie to join them, causing her to feel excluded. She was beginning to feel like a nonperson.

Connie acknowledged that she was feeling embarrassed talking to a therapist about all this; she felt it all sounded silly. With encouragement and support she described her problems in more detail, focusing on the difficulties of modifying the defiant attitudes and behaviors of several of the residents. It was clear that this was part of an unhealthy system with very ambiguous boundaries.

Rather self-consciously, Connie talked about feeling badly about being overweight and aware of looking younger than her age, which she was afraid caused her clients to ignore her instructions. Her insecurity was compounded by inconsistent support from the administration and by the fact that she was frequently left to fend for herself. Often she was not included on trips taken by other staff members and was left to take care of a client who was especially fearful and withdrawn. She resented being the "housebound" staff member, left to care for difficult clients.

In listening to Connie's painful story, her therapist was aware of powerful systemic issues. He wondered also about her own history and her self-cohesion. Was her sense of depletion something new, related to a difficult professional situation, or was it rooted in historical family of origin issues or issues of self-esteem? Where should the treatment focus?

He began by exploring with Connie the problems in the work system. It seemed that the basic problem was Connie's sense of being excluded by the overly close relationship between her partner and her partner's mother. She said it reminded her how she felt when she was last to be chosen for softball teams growing up. Since Connie had never talked to her colleagues about what she was feeling, she was coached in therapy to express some of her feelings to them in a nonreactive way, that is, calmly and directly. (One of the things that so often defeats our efforts to get our feelings heard is that, after holding them in for a long time, we express them in a reactive manner, with such emotional pressure that a defensive reaction from listeners is almost inevitable.) Connie was able to express her feelings rather than vent them and, much to her surprise and pleasure, her coworkers responded quite positively. This led to her being invited to a party given by her coworker, as well as increased social interaction. Initially, she felt much better and quite encouraged by these changes. At first glance, when she changed the way she interacted within the system, things improved dramatically.

However, these changes were short-lived and Connie's symptoms continued, leaving her frustrated and confused. Why, she asked her therapist, was she still feeling so badly when things were improving at work? Her therapist, remembering the story about softball, inquired about what her life was like growing up. She told of not being allowed to have candy because her mother was obsessed with tooth decay. She recalled an incident when she was in the first grade. When Connie came home from a friend's birthday party with a little bag of candy, her mother took it away, saying, "All that junk will rot your teeth!" She went on to say how her home life was filled with chores; she seemed always to be cleaning the house, with little time to play. She explained that her mother got colon cancer when she was 14 and died when she was 16. Connie appeared to be on the verge of tears as she told the story. Her mother failed to respond to several different courses of chemotherapy; she gradually lost weight until she reached 79 pounds. Connie, the youngest child by many years, was the main caretaker of her mother, as her older sister and one older brother lived out of state with their families and the oldest brother was a trucker, frequently on the road. When asked what her mother was like, she said, "Looking back, I would have to say she was cold."

Connie added that she could not recall her father ever working. Her mother was the sole support of the household, working long hours inspecting shoes on an assembly line. Overtime was a necessity to make ends meet. Her father, on the other hand, seemed to live in front of the TV. Although she had no memories of physical abuse, she was terrified of him because he had an explosive temper and could be so cruel. Her self-imposed role was to try to keep things on an even keel so that he would not explode. She recalled being hit only once, when, she said, "I deserved it."

After her mother's death, Connie went to live with her sister in another state, finishing high school with mostly C's and a few D's. She felt unpopular and had few friends, but learned to feel needed by listening to her classmates' problems. Others found it easy to confide in her. After high school graduation she went to live with her father, who died six months later of a heart attack. Connie cried when her father died but thought now that the tears were more for her own lost childhood than for him. At the funeral Connie felt a little guilty when people expressed sympathy for her loss. The truth was, she didn't feel much grief. Her father had been dead to her for a long time.

When the therapist asked Connie about her memories of life before her mother's death, she told of having to baby-sit from ages 10 to 14 for her brother's two small children. Her brother was a truck driver, away from home much of the time. His wife had gone back to work on second shift, leaving Connie as the primary caretaker of the two children from the time she left school until her father picked her up at 9 p.m. Even her summers were given over to childcare. While her friends were out swimming and riding their bikes, Connie was stuck looking after her niece and nephew. When she asked why she had to do this, her parents told her, "Family has to help family!" When asked what happened to her childhood, Connie answered quietly, "I never had one."

Perhaps Connie chose to work with children as an adult because of this earlier caretaking experience; perhaps she was trying to make a virtue out of what had been a necessity. As we have seen, people have an uncanny ability to find work environments in which they can work through unresolved family of origin issues.

While exploring the history of her complaint of nausea, Connie recalled a time when she was nine and felt a wave of nausea come over her: "I felt sick all over. I thought I was going to die. I cried deep down inside (so it wouldn't show) for two days." She went on to tell the following story. Her mother had her collect all her toys, games, and stuffed animals, and place them in paper bags. Connie was puzzled but also intrigued. Her mother then told her, "You're grown-up now, so you can't play with these anymore." They were all given away to neighborhood children. Telling this story, Connie slowly swallowed, with a sickly, disgusted look on her face. "You had no say?" the therapist asked. Connie responded painfully, "I never had any say."

This unforgettable trauma rocked her to the core. This scene was emblematic of other incidents recurring throughout her life. One might wonder how Connie survived. Perhaps she survived through the good-enough parenting she received from her brothers and sister, 12, 15 and 17 years older, who could offer her a place of refuge apart from her parents. Connie believed that her parents wanted to be done with parenting. They often reminded her that she was unplanned.

As Connie explored these painful memories, she recognized the profound similarity of her family history to her current feeling state and circumstances. With support and articulation of her options in weekly therapy over several months, she eventually found another job. This was a step in the right direction.

Connie's story illustrates how a precarious sense of self can play out in the workplace and with contemporary relationships and how the system can exacerbate the tendency to enfeeble an already insecure worker. It would have been a mistake to focus only on clarifying and renegotiating her role and function at work, however useful this might have been. Focusing only on practical problem-solving in the present would have neglected important developmental and psychodynamic aspects of her current adaptation. On the other hand, it would have been a mistake to focus on her tragic past and inability to cope in stressful circumstances without considering a change of those circumstances. We would concede that sometimes merely removing the pebble from the shoe is all that is required for relief. This case required understanding forces from the past and explaining their recapitulation in the present. For example, being left in the residential facility with the frightened adolescent was similar to baby-sitting for her niece and nephew 27 years earlier, while her friends/coworkers were "outside having fun." It was also essential to acknowledge that her present situation was not fair and that extricating herself might be the most expedient remedy.

The story of Myra, a social worker we interviewed at a psychotherapy convention, provides another example of the need for a broad-based analysis of professional overload. Myra is one of those energetic people who made others feel more alive just being in her presence. She has dark wavy hair and a pretty face, but it was her intense and intelligent eyes that drew our attention when we talked to her. Upbeat and interested in what we had to say, she seemed to have it all together.

During our interview she offered the following story. She had actually come to this convention in hopes of becoming professionally rejuvenated. She said that over time she had moved from being physically tired to being emotionally exhausted and finally to being on the verge of a complete breakdown. Her work had come to feel overwhelming. She had tried to deal with her discouragement by seeking psychotherapy. Naturally, where else would a psychotherapist turn for professional help? Her psychotherapy focused on problems with self-esteem that had contributed to her overextending herself for her clients, leading to increased hours at work. Working on these issues brought about some changes and improvements, but only for a while.

She then discovered an unattended problem in another system: her marriage. During a conversation with her husband about her possibly going back to school, she realized that he still expected her to have dinner on the table every night, wash the dishes, match his socks, and drive the kids everywhere they need to go, even if he had nothing more pressing to do than watch Monday night football. Because of his passive resistance, negotiating every task was a struggle. In her therapy, while Myra initially identified self-esteem issues as they related to her work situation as the problem, the "marital system" was significantly contributing to her stress level. Unless the marital issues were brought into the discussion, her therapy would probably not be successful in reversing burnout.

Scott, an alcoholism counselor, sought therapy for depression. He believed that he was in a midlife crisis and that the major contributing stress in his life was his work setting. He identified a variety of things that were wrong at work and attempted to fix them by changing his approach, trying first one thing then another. When this didn't work, he took a new job and was happy for a while. Just as he thought he had solved his problems, they recurred.

Like many clients, early in therapy Scott wanted to work on problem-solving. He hoped that, if he found the right job or at least developed more effective interpersonal strategies to use at work, he would feel better. His evaluations repeatedly mentioned his difficulty getting along with coworkers; moreover, a number of clients complained that he was too pushy and opinionated in therapy. Only after repeated problem-solving strategies failed was he ready to look more deeply at what he might be contributing to the problem. He began slowly to move from an external focus to more internal one. As Scott continued with his therapy he revealed his deep-seated insecurity and gradually uncovered painful memories of early childhood physical abuse. His response to abuse was basically an adaptive one, overcoming his sense of passivity and helplessness by becoming a very active, take-charge kind of person. However, like many strategies that are compensatory, this one was a little rigid. He felt compelled to be active and practical and in charge, and was too anxious to sit back and listen, to let his clients delve into their unhappy experiences, or to let them discover their own meaning and solutions. In this case the client's selection of where to focus failed, at least initially, to identify one of the most significant sources of his problem.

DUCK-RABBITS AND PARADIGMS

Self psychology views interpersonal experience through the subjective lens of the self, while the systems approach views the self through the matrix of the system. While the two theories might initially appear contradictory, they are simply different lenses through which to view the complexity of human experience. As with Wittgenstein's (1973, p. 194) "duck-rabbit," what we see depends on the frame around it (Figure 2). If a vertical frame is put around the "duck-rabbit," it will be seen as a rabbit; if a horizontal frame is put around the same drawing it will be seen as duck. Various frames allow different aspects of reality to be perceived.

Taken together the conceptual frames of self psychology and systems theory allow us to understand both the intrapsychic and subjective aspects of human experience, as well as the interpersonal and systems aspects of human behavior, and how the two interact. Our goal is not to provide a thorough integration of the two theories, but to see how the two theoretical frames illuminate our understanding of burnout, and how they are inextricably connected.

Burnout occurs when several factors converge. Developmentally, many mental health professionals did not receive the right kind of attention growing up. Healthy narcissism was not sufficiently reinforced, and an important need for validation was not met. As we have described in some detail, this insufficient validation of the self at times results in the masking of narcissism (or in the formation of an encapsulated archaic narcissism) that in adulthood manifests as a craving for attention or as a depleted self, which feels both intense psychological pain and helplessness within the system of which it is a part.

Figure 2: Is it a duck or a rabbit? (Reproduced with permission from Blackwell Publishers)

The family system may have also encouraged the child to play a selfobject role for his or her parents, thus reversing normal selfobject functioning (Lee, 1988).

As shown in the Timberlawn research (Beavers & Hampson, 1990; Lewis, Beavers, Gossett, & Phillips, 1976), in healthy families parents form a strong working alliance, an executive subsystem that lets kids know that they are free to be kids, because their needs will be met by the parental subsystem. Such developmentally appropriate boundaries help children feel secure. In dysfunctional families boundaries may be absent or violated; in fact, parent-child roles are often reversed. Rather than receiving the mirroring they desperately need for the formation of healthy and cohesive selves, children wind up needing to provide mirroring for their parents.

Tim, for example, described how he had to do much of the cooking and childcare in his family at a very early age because his alcoholic parents were often incapacitated. At the same time, he felt pressured to reassure his mother that she was doing a great job. The only appreciation he received was for performing heroic roles in taking care of his siblings and parents, thus reinforcing his overfunctioning role. His mother often bragged to her friends about how responsible he was. She also took great pleasure in showing his report cards to her friends, but this showing-off didn't make Tim feel appreciated, since he could tell it was her way of boasting about her own accomplishments as a mother.

Too often, praise for performance, such as Tim received, becomes internalized in the form of a belief that if the child were not to take charge and play out the role a catastrophe would result. Unfortunately, repeatedly there may have been truth in that belief. The belief system is repeatedly reinforced as the family is rescued from yet another crisis by the child's efforts. Consequently, the belief system gains power and eventually becomes a core organizing belief.

Obviously, not all mental health professionals played the role of parental child in their families. This is but one example of how an excessive need for mirroring or admiration can have its beginnings in family of origin experience, and have a great impact on later functioning. Old roles are not easily unlearned. As adults we define ourselves to the world much as we did as children. Thus we may find it very difficult to set appropriate boundaries, say no when necessary, or set limits on our work, if we continue performing as heroic children.

Work systems are by no means neutral. The system isn't a blank slate on which we write our personal scripts; it is an active and dynamic set of influences that shapes and sometimes bends us. It may be short on staff, with long client waiting lists. Good supportive supervision may not be available, and the supervision offered may be more critical than helpful. Therapists who have not received appropriate mirroring in family of origin may find it difficult to set boundaries within this difficult system, just as they found it impossible to do so as children. Rather than define themselves nonreactively to the system, they get caught in the various feedback loops; instead of learning to say no to extra hours they volunteer to take extra clients as a way of reducing waiting lists; rather than becoming assertive and pushing for extra secretarial help, they volunteer to do their own paperwork.

Without a cohesive self (Kohut) or a high degree of differentiation of self (Bowen), the individual will have a hard time assertively defining himself or herself amidst destructive pressures in the work system. Kohut and Bowen were both concerned with how the self responds to external systems. They examine the nature of that response, however, from different perspectives. Kohut emphasized individual development in terms of how one's early environment was experienced, as well as one's current need for selfobject experience. Bowen emphasized multigenerational family processes, with differentiation of self as the central theme. Both therapists, however, looked at the system from the subjective lens of the individual. This becomes an important issue in relating to work systems. For many helping professionals, it is all too easy to see the work environment as a substitute family and to overwork in an attempt to receive mirroring—or what Allen (1979) refers to as consensual validation. Rewards may come from clients and their idealizing transference, or from administrators who are quick to praise overwork. However, these are seldom enough. The hunger for mirroring and the inability to find it in many work environments are the primary cause of professional burnout.

Many work systems have the characteristics of dysfunctional families. Boundaries are unclear, administrators act like inconsistent parents, workloads are unrealistic, support staff are few or nonexistent, office space is not only unattractive but at times quite uncomfortable. Working in these work environments may leave one feeling stressed from a number of angles.

Sarah, a junior faculty member at a small private college, told her therapist of being abused and harassed by a tyrannical department chairman. He yelled at her when he disagreed with something she was doing or, God forbid, if she ever dared challenge something he said. The only way he seemed to accept her was as docile and accommodating. At first she tried to avoid his temper and stay in his good graces. But even his good graces turned out to be trouble, because he went from complimenting her on her appearance to touching her under the guise of admiring what she was wearing. The academic system she described tolerated a department chair who, like a bad parent, violated the boundaries of those he oversaw.

Sarah was paralyzed by ambivalence. The department chair was so reminiscent of her strong but aloof mother that Sarah found herself caught between anger and the desire to please him. In therapy she came to realize that, while with her mother being extra good might pay off while being demanding never did, she was no longer a child and her boss wasn't her mother. She didn't need to placate him, and she didn't need to protect him. Once she realized this, she could decide to no longer suffer his abuse in silence. Unlike when she was a child, there *was* someplace she could go for help. She was helped to see how she was conditioned to try to please him. It then became more possible for her to tolerate and stand up to his outbursts. She was also helped to be wary of compliments about her appearance when they became overly personal from people she didn't really have a personal relationship with or know she could trust to respect personal boundaries. She declined to respond like a child and instead acted like a responsible, mature adult in defending herself and her professional reputation. Ultimately, she exemplified healthy self-definition in response to an unhealthy system.

Cliff, a social worker and team leader at a mental health center, comes for therapy complaining of chronic fatigue and burnout. He reports feeling numb and states that he is only going through the motions on his job. He describes staring into space in the mornings while at his desk and dreading all the clients he has to face the rest of the day. He is not at all sure that going back into therapy will help, but feels he has to do *something*. He is beginning to wonder whether he is in the right position, even in the right profession.

Cliff was the oldest of five children in a close-knit, perfectionistic family. His father was demanding and difficult to please. In childhood, even when he would bring home a good report card, his father would point out how it could have been better. He felt pressured by both parents to be the one who excelled in the family, and he had a sense that his mother lived vicariously through him. She went to work on a factory assembly line at an early age to help out her family and always regretted not going to college herself. He could not recall being able to relax, even play much with friends in the neighborhood, since he was always striving to get high grades.

Now he sees his parents infrequently and feels like a child when he is with them. He acknowledges that he is still trying to earn his father's approval. He usually asks his father if he needs any help with household repairs, even though his dad has always been the better handyman. He also feels estranged from his wife and two adolescent children and says that his wife neither understands nor appreciates him and is constantly critical of him. He feels distant from his kids.

On the other hand, he relates that for at least the first ten years in his present position he loved the work and even put in hours way beyond what was expected. He says it gave him a sense of meaning and purpose to be of help to people, and admits that he is a people pleaser and enjoys getting people to like him. Lately, however, many of his staff have been calling in sick, while his director has been complaining about his team's decline in units of service as well as rate of collections. He recently was criticized because several members of his team have been delinquent in their record keeping. He has always hated checking charts to see if his staff were keeping up with their workload.

Cliff thought his hard work (and that of others as well) was primarily a matter of ideals and professionalism, but the real engine that drove him was wanting to be liked. When he turned to his wife, Martha, and children, Jenny, 17, and Michael, 15, for support, he found them cold and critical. This left him hurt and frustrated, but he was unable to realize how he contributed to their detached attitude. His long hours at the clinic, along with an expanding part-time private practice, had left his family bitter and distant. The more he gave to his work, the more it seemed to consume him. His current fantasies were to meet another woman who would understand him and give him the affection he "deserved" and to find a new agency that would "appreciate" him. At the same time, he realized that the problem is more complex.

Cliff had all the signs and symptoms of burnout: chronic fatigue, feeling numb, loss of meaning and purpose, easy distractibility, feelings of dread about the day and tasks at hand, feelings of hopelessness, doubts about his competence and even choice of career.

Not surprisingly, family of origin exploration revealed a generational pattern of lack of warmth and nurturing behavior. Cliff remembered with some anger how delighted his mother would become when he won awards at school. He did not mind her initial enthusiasm but grew increasingly uncomfortable when she would repeatedly ask him to tell her friends about his accomplishments. His father, on the other hand, would remain reserved; he would always find something to criticize and push him to do better. Cliff referred to his mother as an emotional cheerleader who lived through him but whose accolades were meaningless, while he remained unclear where he stood with his father. This would suggest some arrested development and lack in his capacity for self-acceptance and self-soothing; perhaps he is "still trying to earn his father's approval." He is externally focused and desperately needs others to make him feel okay.

Because of the disconnection in his current family and his spouse's lack of response, he feels all the more unsupported and insecure. His family has unwittingly replicated the lack of mirroring and nurturing experienced in his family of origin. His current family does not feel like a safe place.

Earlier in his career he had ambition, initiative, and idealism. He derived meaning from his work. However, he may have been too dependent on being liked and appreciated by others, to compensate for what he did not receive as a child. Unfortunately, but all too commonly, the circumstances of his work environment became less and less supportive, and more and more demanding, due to budget cutbacks and resultant staff shortages. Because of his need to be liked, he did not have any way of defining himself appropriately in his work system and learning to be assertive with people who reported to him (recall his avoidance of staff record keeping). Had he been less anxious at work, and able to set firmer limits and boundaries as opposed to taking on more and more work in order to be liked, things might have been different. However, the frustrations and disappointment at work poisoned his attitude, which he then carried home. He failed to recognize how he had come to antagonize his family. He sought more positive self-enhancing selfobject experiences by expanding his private practice, which resulted in even less time at home. Initially this satisfied him and increased his income; some of his clients idealized him. However, as his practice expanded so did the criticism at home, as well as the pressures at the agency. He resorted to fantasies of love and how the grass would be greener if he were to move, start a lucrative private practice, and meet a new woman.

Cliff's burnout, a classic case, can be understood from the various perspectives we've been considering. From the perspective of his need for a cohesive self, he is lacking some capacity for self-acceptance and self-soothing, as well as the ability to utilize healthy (mature) selfobjects. As a result of his propensity to reinforce a fragile self by overworking, he has become caught in a series of feedback loops. The harder he worked, the more reinforcement he received, buttressing his fragile sense of self; however, he could never be liked enough at work. His wife and children were critical of him for his disengagement from their lives; their anger pushed him away even when he sought closeness. He was unable to differentiate or define himself appropriately either at work and in his family. He could not set realistic limits and seek appropriate support at work. Nor could he listen openly, objectively, and without defensiveness to his family's complaints. We could also see his burnout as a multigenerational pattern, the result of carrying the "mantle" for generations in his family, combined with family rules about not expressing conflict.

According to Nichols (1987), a therapist who works with both individual experience and contemporary interactional forces must shift focus to concentrate sometimes on the system and sometimes on the self. Alternating perspectives, the clinician can move across models to effect change. Because "the system" and "the self" are, in fact, only different ways to describe people's lives, one cannot separate them; each model is more or less useful in different circumstances. The inner world or state of the self echoes the external dependence the individual has on the people to whom he or she is attached. Self and object are fundamentally interdependent. Interpersonal events and objects link with unconscious motivations to bring about selfobject experiences that vitalize the self. When there is a breakdown or selfobject failure, the joys of selfhood fade into empty depression and burnout.

Professionals look at their work systems through the lens of their unique belief system or cognitive appraisal, which is frequently unconscious. Cognitive blinders, the legacy of family of origin issues, may keep them from defining themselves assertively and creatively and setting boundaries. How many times do we hear ourselves saying, "Yes, I'd be glad to," when everything within us is screaming that we are already overextended? This painfully exemplifies how the cognitive appraisal of systems and events at work results from lack of self-esteem or replication of old family roles. When we lose the ability to define ourselves in a healthy manner to the variety of systems in which we are involved, we are at risk for burnout.

5

PREVENTION: AVOIDING BURNOUT

Overwork is the curse of our time. Working long hours has become almost a badge of honor among professional people, whose complaints about overwork are often mixed with a sense of pride in their dedication and importance—and perhaps a sense of entitlement, namely that their hard work justifies avoidance and indulgence in other areas of their lives. Nowhere is this ethos of overwork more prevalent than in the helping professions, where the overwhelming demand for service has made long hours expected and honored. These days it seems that every time you ask fellow mental health professionals how they're doing, you're likely to hear how busy they are and how little time they have for things other than work. Unfortunately, neither the familiarity nor apparent meritoriousness of chronic busyness keeps it from leading, more and more often, to a gradual and permanent depletion of the spirit.

Burnout is reaching epidemic proportions in the helping professions. It is an insidious and complex problem caused not by any one factor but by a combination of environmental and work circumstances, emptiness and drivenness, and an exaggerated need to shore up the self at the expense of real communion with friends and family. More specifically, as we have shown, it can be understood from a variety of theoretical frames, including self psychology, general systems theory, and the multigenerational perspective of Murray Bowen.

It is one thing to describe the experience of burnout and to provide a theoretical explanation; it is quite another to prevent it. Yet, it obviously makes more sense to avoid burnout than to try to rebuild the lives and spirits of its victims after the fact.

All too often, when mental health workers attend conferences or seminars on preventing burnout or dealing with stress, they receive simplistic formulas and advice: exercise more, develop outside interests and hobbies, balance work and play. Such advice is easier to give than to follow. Unfortunately, such common sense solutions usually do not work, and frequently leave people feeling even more frustrated and guilty. Not only are they worn out, but they have failed Relaxation 101.

On the other hand, many professionals pursue relaxation seriously and take up tennis, or running, or some other hobby. The problem is that they become just as compulsive about leisure time activities as they have been about their work. One psychotherapist became very discouraged with his biking after realizing that he could never go out for a relaxing bike ride; rather he felt pressured (by no one but himself) to bike longer and faster each trip. Another took up running as a form of stress reduction. This worked well until she began keeping track of how many miles she ran each day and trying to increase the mileage she ran each week, until she reached 65 miles a week. Whenever she skipped a day of running, she felt guilty; eventually, however, knee problems forced her to reduce training. In both of these cases, the solution became part of the problem.

While passions for new activities or fantasies of new lives or careers in more exciting communities are a normal part of life, they can serve as distractions from what feels like overwhelming emptiness or as selfobjects upon which we become dependent for internal cohesion. How many of us have not had fantasies of very different professions in new communities, perhaps with a new spouse or family? At times the fantasies serve to distance us from the difficulty of changing the unpleasant realities of the present. However, neither fantasies nor new activities are able to help people with the major business of life: love and work. Nor do they change one's personality. If one is driven to achieve at work, then one may be equally driven at a new sport or hobby. If one has difficulty setting boundaries and saying no at work, then the same problem is likely to arise in group-related hobbies or volunteer work. For instance, a social worker who sought to balance his life by getting more involved in his church found that, just as he had difficulty saying no at work, he could not say no to requests to serve on committees at church.

The professional's new hobbies may leave family members more frustrated than ever. The spouse who complains about her husband's long hours in a mental health clinic and loss of family intimacy is going to be less than enthusiastic about his attempt to bring balance into his life by playing golf every weekend, leaving her to care for their small children. Solutions that fail to take into account family issues, as well as the personality issues and narcissistic vulnerabilities of those in the helping professions, and that ignore the enormous difficulties of working in the mental health system, are doomed to failure. If the way in which many mental health professionals replicate family dynamics at work is not addressed, or if they are not helped to understand why setting boundaries and saying no are so important, efforts to prevent burnout will not work.

Obviously, a theory of prevention must take seriously personality issues within the professional, wrestle with the complexities of working in the mental health system, and help the professional find ways of defining him or herself within that system, as well as finding balance and meaning in life. Several important steps can be taken that may help prevent burnout. These include realistic self-assessment, investigation of the impact of one's family of origin, understanding one's own narcissistic issues, utilizing support groups, finding effective supervision, and finally, finding balance in one's life.

RECOGNIZING THE SIGNS OF BURNOUT: SELF-ASSESSMENT

Spotting the signs of burnout is rarely as easy as it sounds. Differentiating normal tiredness, tension, and occasional exhaustion from the gradual debilitation of burnout is difficult. Consider these two cases: Nancy, executive director of a not-for-profit counseling center, reported feeling exhausted and constantly tense as a result of attempting to make massive changes in her agency to better prepare it to negotiate the complexities of the managed care maze. Yet, after interviewing her, we felt sure that she was not in the early stages of burnout. Beneath her tiredness and tension we sensed a clear resilience that kept her energized and moving toward some clear goals. Her optimism was evident. Despite the pressure to make the massive changes necessary in her agency, she addressed it creatively and constructively. While Nancy was tense and tired, she could see light at the end of the tunnel and was enthusiastic about getting there. She bravely led her agency through some renewed strategic planning, working towards the accomplishment of clear short-term goals, all aimed at necessary change for the agency. For her, stress became a constructive challenge which helped her stretch and expand. Nancy was able to sustain her hard work because her job allowed her creativity, self-expression, self-esteem, and feelings of security.

Nancy is an example of someone for whom stress became a constructive challenge. Others experience stress, particularly the type over which we have little creative control or relief, as progressively wearing them down. When we talked with Seth, clinical director at another agency, this was the type of picture that emerged. His apathy and total lack of enthusiasm were almost palpable. While Seth shared Nancy's exhaustion and anxiety, he did not have her optimism or future vision, just a dark and dreary sense that his spirit had been broken. He felt alone and unsupported in making changes in his agency, and felt a total absence of personal control and creativity in coping with his agency's problems. His executive director offered no help or support, and Seth felt that any effort towards change was like banging his head into a brick wall. Nancy's tiredness could be dealt with by setting some goals, taking a few long weekends and perhaps a good vacation. Seth's burnout would be more difficult to treat.

If burnout is to be prevented, professionals must learn to distinguish between normal tiredness or tension and the early signs of burnout. Ongoing self-assessment will help them recognize both the early stages of burnout and signs of their susceptibility to it.

Self-assessment in this case has several levels. On the first surface level, helping professionals need to periodically scan their experience, using their observing ego to transcend themselves and their experience and realistically assess how they are doing in several areas of their lives. This involves questioning how much enjoyment and satisfaction they are getting from their work, as well as checking for feelings of enthusiasm and optimism. It includes being sensitive to feelings of dread of going to work, or excessive boredom, or feelings of flatness, tiredness, and pessimism about the future. It means being aware of how often they fantasize about finding a new position or even a new career. These fantasies are often related to perceiving some sense of personal control and a sense that their talents are being put to use in a way that leads to a sense of feeling appreciated. In addition, it means assessing the balance in their activities, and whether they are becoming one-dimensional, thinking, reading, and studying only what is relevant to their profession and neglecting different interests, people, and ideas. Finally, it means honestly assessing their family life, how their spouse and children are doing, and how they fit in the daily family system. Asking for feedback from the spouse and children can be revealing.

Sometimes this assessment is depressing in itself, because just looking at all these variables may in itself be overwhelming. We need to be aware of our own resilience and ability to bounce back from tiredness. Runners, for example, learn quickly about the dangers of overtraining. They learn the hard way that ignoring injuries or trying to push training to a more intense level simply invites more serious problems. As a result, if they are to be successful as athletes, they learn to differentiate the signs of overtraining from simply training hard. Signs of overtraining for the athlete are fairly obvious: loss of the joy of the sport, feeling of deadness, dread of training, declining performance, sluggishness and fatigue, insomnia or sleep disturbance, weight changes, greater susceptibility to colds and flu, irritability, lack of zest, and shortened attention span—to name a few. The parallels to burnout at work are obvious. On the other hand, runners frequently find that cutting back on training or cross training (bike riding, swimming, lifting weights) often restores enthusiasm. If it doesn't, more serious interventions are called for.

In a similar fashion, when mental health professionals begin to feel flat, tired, or bored, or report many of the same types of symptoms athletes report when they have overtrained, they may try "cross training." This may involve study leaves, conferences, reading novels, getting away for a long weekend or vacation, or rearranging schedules to allow for hobbies. But perhaps the best idea—and most like cross training—would be varying the jobs they do at work. While most bosses are less than enthusiastic about staff refusing assignments, most are quite receptive to staff who initiate requests to try different things. If this works, it is fair to assume that tiredness or perhaps a very early stage of burnout was the problem. If it does not work and feelings of apathy, flatness, and irritability continue, then burnout is more than likely the culprit. People who are burning out do not usually bounce back.

Distinguishing, in self-assessment, between burnout and tiredness can be difficult. Symptoms of burnout could simply mean that a vacation is long overdue; a couple of weeks on a beach might reverse the feelings. It could mean that one needs more variety or flexibility at work. It could also indicate that marital and family problems are exacerbating work-related stress. Self-assessment may identify proactive steps that can be taken to prevent burnout. For example, an alcoholism counselor was able to reverse early burnout by becoming more selectively involved at work. She was able to increase her control by cutting out things that were optional and no longer (if ever) rewarding. She took herself off a few committees. She reinvested in her clinical work by starting up a special therapy group, which turned out to be greatly satisfying, even exciting. She said she felt better because she had expanded the scope of her effectiveness.

If, however, symptoms persist, then a more advanced stage of burnout should be diagnosed. One of the sure signs of burnout is when weekends and vacations don't restore. When you come back without feeling refreshed, it may be a sign, not that you need a longer break, but that something more than just a break is needed. At this point, one needs to move assessment to two additional levels: family of origin issues, and one's own narcissistic vulnerability.

FAMILY OF ORIGIN WORK

When we address significant problems in our lives, we naturally focus on where the hurt is. We want the pain to go away quickly. In the case of professional burnout, we zero in on our disillusionment with work, or on our exhaustion, or maybe on the disappointments or strain on our home life and the way they compound our work stress. In the midst of this pain, the idea of examining the way in which the families we grew up in influenced our roles and scripts for living may seem far removed from the primary problem. Unfortunately, not examining those issues in the interest of solving the problem quickly is much like putting a band-aid on an injury that needs more thorough attention. The imprint of our families sets up both roles and unconscious expectations that continue to be played out in our marriages and in our work environments. Only when these patterns, roles, and unconscious expectations are understood and dealt with can we avoid getting trapped in narrow and self defeating approaches to love and work.

Psychoanalytic training has historically stressed the need for a training analysis as an integral part of the therapist's development, while Bowenian training has emphasized the need for therapists to resolve unfinished business with their families in order to develop mature objectivity. While it may not be necessary for all helping professionals to undergo depth analysis or even Bowen's family of origin work, it may be very helpful for those whose neurotic problems begin to cause problems in their work—or where work brings forth neurotic problems.

The best way to begin exploring the family that shaped you is to make a genogram of your family. Whether you use the formal procedure for drawing a genogram, as outlined by McGoldrick and Gerson (1985), or invent your own method of tracking your family tree is not important. What is important is that you find some way of considering and tracking at least three generations and of taking into account key dates and events in family history, as well as the major conflicts and triangles, in order to understand the family legacy operating in your life.

Using either a genogram or your own informal family map as a springboard, you can begin to explore several important issues. The goal is not an exhaustive review of family themes but rather a simple understanding of several key issues. One important theme to consider involves the family rules about dealing with conflict. Was open conflict permitted? If so, what were the rules of engagement? Was it okay to argue? To raise your voice? Or was it imperative to remain "calm" and "be reasonable"? Was challenging your parents allowed? Fighting with your siblings? All these questions have obvious relevance for how one handles conflict at work.

If in one's family of origin arguing was not allowed and no tools for dealing with conflict were developed, then one will avoid confrontation and find it difficult to be appropriately assertive. The boy who didn't learn to fight in the family becomes a man who doesn't know how to stand up for himself at work; the girl who learned that being "good" (long suffering) was the way to get rewarded may discover that this strategy doesn't work very well for grown-ups. Learning to say no and to set firm boundaries about how much responsibility to take on at work is hard enough for most of us. Those who grew up in families where there was no example of assertiveness or healthy confrontation find it even more difficult.

Another important family legacy pertains to the spoken or unspoken rules about the value of work. Was overwork encouraged and rewarded? Were you encouraged even as a child to believe that achievement or selfless dedication was more important than having fun? Or, even if children in your family were allowed to be children, did either or both of your parents set an example of all work and no play? Many mental health professionals recall hearing messages throughout childhood about the need to do things perfectly, and so end up compulsively following that message in their careers. For others, whose families lived through depressing economic times, overwork can become a way of dealing with the anxieties of past generations. Ironically, those of us who were favored in our families or scripted to be "the successful one" often feel the mantle of success as a burden. Living up to the legacy of being the successful or favored child can become exhausting, and it is easy to feel driven by something bigger than ourselves. Bowen called the process whereby a theme or role is passed on over several generations "multigenerational transmission" (1978, p. 477).

Other professionals will find in exploring their family histories that there were consistent messages, given out both subtly and not so subtly, about perfectionism and the need to be compulsive about doing things right. This script frequently plays out in compulsive overfunctioning and a need to do everything perfectly, without always knowing the source of that anxiety. Discovering in ourselves neurotic habits that turn out to be like our parents' can make us feel fatalistic and discouraged. But sometimes just seeing ourselves playing out certain scripted roles can inspire us to experiment with changing the script.

Finally, in some families, work functions like an addiction that prevents underlying emptiness from manifesting itself. Like other addictions, overwork tends to be passed on generationally. Just as in alcoholic families the pattern of problem drinking is seen over several generations, so in workaholic families the pattern of problem working is present, as Diane Fassell notes in her book *Working Ourselves to Death*. This predilection for overwork is particularly common in families who have experienced substantial loss, economic depression, or financial reversals. Here work can function much like an addiction, covering much emptiness and pain.

Patterns of overfunctioning and underfunctioning in the family of origin should also be tracked. Systems theory suggests that there is a predictable feedback loop between over- and underfunctioning. Whenever one person in a family underfunctions, someone else will overfunction to compensate. The more one overfunctions, the more the other will underfunction, and vice versa. In dysfunctional families, parents frequently do not take charge in appropriate ways, which sets up a pattern of underfunctioning. This results in someone, usually one of the children, having to overfunction. Thus, for example, a girl who grows up with a mother who often seems depressed or overburdened may take over much of the housework or looking after her brothers and sisters. The child is parentified and does far more than is appropriate or even reasonable. This pattern of overfunctioning is not easily overcome, not only because it's familiar, but also because it is so well rewarded. Too often it reappears in work settings, which all too easily become yet another family and a new arena for overfunctioning. As in families, the more one overfunctions at work, the more one's coworkers will underfunction. Overfunctioning at work is particularly common, because for every person ready to do more than his or her share there are several others quite willing to do less.

Much of the literature on adult children of alcoholic families talks about the roles that children play in their families that reinforce overfunctioning (Black, 1982; Jesse, 1989, 1990; Woititz, 1983). One role that receives much attention is that of the hero or rescuer in the family. The hero is the overfunctioning member of the family who goes out of his or her way to take care of everyone else. Unfortunately, this well-intended generosity is usually performed at great expense, resulting in the loss of freedom to be a "real self." The "hero" tends to replay this same role at work, leading at times to burnout. Part of prevention is understanding how these problematic roles stay with us and keep us overfunctioning in work environments so that we are pushed increasingly closer to burnout, driven by the fear that something terrible will happen if we slow down.

The first steps in prevention, then, are to understand the messages we received in our families, comprehend patterns of overfunctioning frequently driven by dysfunctional family structure, and clarify the roles that were played in the family. Only by understanding these patterns and the ways they are replicated in current work situations can we begin to prevent burnout.

In a workshop on repetition of family of origin themes, Ann said that in her family of origin she was the good child. Her parents constantly rewarded her for compliance and held her up to her four other siblings as a model to be emulated. This left Ann in a grave predicament. On the one hand, she enjoyed the constant positive feedback from her parents, which enhanced her self-esteem. On the other, her siblings came to resent her and distance from her for being so good. She found herself trying to apologize to them for her favored status. Now she finds herself in the same bind as a school social worker. She enjoys the many accolades she receives from her supervisors, and has been singled out as a positive role model for entry-level social workers. Increasingly anxious in this role, she finds herself apologizing to her coworkers for her favored status. She is now continually uptight about work and feels in a constant no-win situation.

In addition to understanding the legacy of our families, Bowenian theory suggests that we need to understand our level of differentiation of self. Differentiation is conceptualized on a scale of 0–100 with 100 representing the totally differentiated person (a theoretical ideal which is never achieved), and 0 representing complete undifferentiation or "no-self." According to Bowen, "The ability to be in emotional contact with others yet still autonomous in one's emotional functioning is the essence of the concept of differentiation" (Kerr & Bowen, 1988, p. 145). Undifferentiated people deal with their families with one of two extremes: cut-off ("the immature separation of people") or fusion ("ways the people borrow or lend a self to another") (Kerr & Bowen, 1988, p. 346). Persons who cut off attempt to stay distant from family and deal with family tensions by having as little contact as possible. Those people who deal with their family by fusion or enmeshment do just the opposite. In response to chronic anxiety, they remain involved in the family, preventing any sense of a differentiated self from emerging.

Differentiated persons can be with the family and still free to be themselves without either cutting off or fusing. They can maintain a sense of what E. Friedman calls non-anxious presence (1985, p. 208). In other relationships they are able to maintain their own identity while at the same time allowing for intimacy without feeling overwhelmed by it. In work settings, they can maintain their own sense of differentiation by maintaining their own sense of self, setting appropriate boundaries, and saying no when necessary. Persons with little differentiation, on the other hand, will have great difficulty setting appropriate boundaries at work and may wind up doing much more than is appropriate. Such persons often claim that when asked to do something unpleasant their head says no but their mouth says yes. They wind up taking on too many responsibilities or tasks for which they do not wish to be responsible.

Assessing our level of differentiation and how it operates both in our family of origin and at work is an important part of prevention. Most of us are conditioned both by Western culture and family experience to think of ourselves as relatively mature and autonomous. It is easy to assume that we are therefore well differentiated. Often only in our thirties do we begin to become aware of the unresolved emotional sensitivities we carry around with us, our reactivity to our parents and others who remind us of them, and our susceptibility to triangling. We begin to realize we are not quite as differentiated as we hoped; we even admit that when we visit our families we feel and act as though we were adolescents again.

What are some of the signs of differentiation? They include being able to have a one-to-one relationship with both parents, and being able to understand the annoying things they do without becoming anxious or reactive. It involves being able to be oneself without significant anxiety, and to talk relatively openly about a wide variety of subjects. It also means being able to separate thinking from feeling and to think about what you are feeling. When we do this we can maintain a calm, nonreactive stance even in the midst of difficult situations, such as those times our parents do those annoying things, that tend to push all of our buttons, or when we are in the midst of one of those staff meetings that deteriorate into blaming and withdrawal.

Since we tend to act without thinking when we are anxious, it is helpful to check what Michael Kerr calls one's "meter for measuring anxiety":

> An individual can develop his own "meter" for measuring anxiety. He can do this by learning to associate particular thoughts, fantasies, dreams, feelings, physical reactions, and behaviors with increases or decreases in his level of anxiety. Techniques such as biofeedback can help a person become more aware of his physical manifestations of anxiety. An individual can learn enough about himself to make fairly accurate judgments about his level of anxiety, but so much variation exists in the way different individuals manage or manifest anxiety that one person's experience is not extrapolated easily to others. Even when people learn about their physical and psychological manifestations of anxiety, they are still vulnerable to ignoring or to misreading signals at critical times. (Kerr & Bowen, 1988, p. 320)

During times of stress or transition, our anxiety is bound to be elevated. Awareness of this can help us step back, look at the big picture, and avoid making bad decisions when our thinking processes have been overwhelmed by our emotions.

Another part of self-assessment involves evaluating how differentiated we are at home and at work. Can we go home and visit our parents and have a one-to-one conversation with each of them, without becoming reactive when they annoy us or engaging in old games? Can we be ourselves and talk about a range of subjects, without hiding who we are or becoming overly defensive? Can we disagree either at home or at work without attacking or remaining mute? Do we find ourselves becoming paralyzed in the face of disagreement, or else unreasonably angry and unable to think clearly?

If in answering these questions we discover that we are not well differentiated, one place to start defining a self is with our family of origin. Building authentic relationships with parents and siblings is very difficult work; it is usually done over a long period of time and often involves one step forward and a half-step back. Coaching from a therapist can help keep us nonreactive when we are pushed to be the way our family remembers us. This work involves giving up the fantasy of changing our family and recognizing that we can change only ourselves, not others. Self-definition is particularly challenging when it involves extricating oneself from pathological triangles. For example, if one parent confides in us all the evils of the other, then getting out of that triangle means not only refusing to continue to listen but also suggesting that one parent talk to the other and not to us—all the while remaining calm and committed to repeating this process many times.

In therapist's-own-family groups professionals wrestle with the impact of their families of origin on their present relationships. This is one context in which mental health professionals can explore patterns of differentiation in both family of origin and work settings and receive some "coaching" as to how to achieve greater differentiation in both places. As mental health professionals achieve greater differentiation, they can define themselves more appropriately in their work systems. This might include learning to set more appropriate boundaries at work, particularly in terms of hours worked and extra assignments accepted. It might also include learning to ask for more compensation or advocate for better working conditions, such as more support staff, better supervision, or additional in-service programs.

Many professionals have discovered in these groups an invaluable resource for growth. Too often it is easy to assume that because we know a great deal about family systems theory, we have achieved a measure of differentiation within our own families. When we finally begin to understand how undifferentiated we are, it is far from easy to make changes. Who has not declared that the next visit home is going to be different, only to find that within hours of getting home we feel and act like we're 15 years old again? Making these changes on our own is next to impossible. The support and coaching of a therapist's-own-family group help us make these types of changes. Through coaching around being nonreactive—that is, not getting "hooked" in predictable ways, getting out of difficult triangles, and building genuine one-to-one relationships with our own relatives—exciting changes can be achieved. These types of changes result in far greater levels of differentiation of self. These changes in turn can generate other types of changes in other systems such as work systems, leading to greater differentiation of self in those systems as well. The unique combination of practical coaching and support that these groups offer can facilitate tremendous changes in differentiation, which can be of enormous value in preventing burnout.

Frequently, in order to optimize work conditions, significant family of origin exploration is necessary. For example, Fred's parents had always talked with great pride about how he had been like an extra parent to his handicapped brother. He was constantly praised for his self-sacrificing ways and for putting his brother's needs ahead of his own. Not surprisingly, in his current work situation he found himself supervising some less capable mental health professionals. He consistently functioned in an overresponsible manner, trying to take care of their needs at the expense of his own schedule, resulting in working more hours than ever. His executive director consistently praised him for his sacrificial style. He came to therapy feeling depressed, tired, and unable to go on any longer. The last straw was that his mother had become quite ill, and so on top of all his work responsibilities he was trying to care for her. Only when his therapist was able to help him see the role he had played, and how he had never separated himself from that role, did he begin to recognize his anger and resentment for all the responsibility he carried. As he examined and worked this through, he was coached by his therapist to slowly begin to differentiate himself from both his family role and his work role and to define himself as an individual.

Obviously, for Fred, insight and initial efforts at differentiation were simply a beginning. Anytime we try and change our role within our family system, the system inevitably responds with subtle and not so subtle messages to change back, making ongoing differentiation quite difficult. This was certainly true in the case of Fred. He experienced growth as two steps forward, followed by one step back (sometimes more than one step!). Whenever he would try to set boundaries as to how often he would go home to help out his parents, he would be left feeling guilty. In a similar way, whenever he began to set boundaries and articulate his needs at work, the same anxious guilt would return. Fred needed the support and coaching of the group, over the course of a year, to slowly stay nonreactive and change a role that had been a major part of his identity. At the same time, he needed not to simply distance from his family, and cut off, but rather to spend quality time with them in a new way, building one-to-one relationships with his parents.

THE COHESIVENESS OF THE SELF: AN ASSESSMENT

In addition to evaluating family of origin issues we must realistically assess our fundamental need for appreciation and meaning, that deep desire to be liked and admired which can easily drive us to overwork.

The subject of narcissism is frequently misunderstood. The very idea of self-love strikes us as selfish and so we tend to overlook or disparage our need to be admired and our right to be proud. In fact, those people we call "narcissistic" are those in whom narcissism miscarries—insecure people whose constant need to call attention to themselves is a sign of self-doubt, not self-love.

The great paradox revealed by professional burnout is that, although helping others can and should be a way to transcend ourselves, many of us embark on helping careers not out of a genuine concern for others but rather out of a need to be appreciated by them. For all too many professional helpers, the real motivation is getting love, not giving it. Kohut's concept of the selfobject again is extremely useful in this discussion. The idealization of dependent clients, admiration of our colleagues, and positive feedback from our supervisors serve selfobject functions in enabling us to feel better about ourselves or, as Kohut put it, to feel more cohesive. As long as we can secure this admiration and feedback by working hard (usually not hard to do since overwork is often rewarded), we will tend to overwork.

Gratification of the idealizing transference can lead to emotional entanglements with clients. Many of the therapists who become sexually involved with their clients do so because they need the idealization of clients to build their own self-esteem; it is easy to confuse this with "love." Dealing with the power of these abusive relationships is not as easy as describing them.

In order to achieve balance and find satisfaction in love and work, we must accept our own need to be appreciated and admired, and then learn how to express it. Working on this issue in isolation can be difficult. While simply gaining insight into this explosive issue can be helpful, it is frequently not enough; consequently, professionals may want to explore several options for further treatment. Individual or group growth-oriented therapy may be one way to come to grips with narcissistic vulnerability. A less intense option would be a safe support group of peers.

Whatever the context for exploration, knowing our vulnerabilities is an important part of self-assessment and prevention. In safe contexts professionals can begin being honest about themselves and sharing their private issues. When professionals are aware of their weaknesses, as well as their desire for appreciation and admiration, they are less likely to begin the slow and painful descent into burnout. They are also less likely to abuse the therapeutic relationship, using it to build their own self-esteem, or to overwork as a way of bolstering their sense of adequacy.

This issue must also be explored in relation to one's present family, particularly one's spouse and children. Rarely do immediate family members provide the type of idealizing admiration and attention that we crave and that certain clients or even colleagues provide. Sean, for example, described with some anger how sick he was of the way his wife refused to "support" him. However, in our conversation it became clear what Sean really craved was not support but admiring attention. He wished to be admired and was angered when his wife saw his flaws. While intellectually he realized that it was unrealistic to expect his wife to see him as wonderful in every way, he admitted that down deep that was what he wanted.

Sean and his wife needed to explore ways of dealing with his narcissistic need in the marriage, before it had further destructive impact. When issues like these are ignored they can cause tremendous pain. When we do not understand and deal with our craving for admiration and need to be seen in given ways, we tend to get angry and resentful. When our kids, instead of telling us what great parents we are, remind us of how we are not meeting their needs, we tend to withdraw. Withdrawal is painful and problematic in two ways: First, it alienates us from our families, which can leave us depressed and lonely; and second, it makes us too dependent on whatever gratification we receive at work.

This calls for some honest self-examination. How much are we avoiding our family's needs, and even our own personal lives, in favor of the personal gratification we get at work? How involved with our family are we? Are we clear about what the needs of those in our family are? Are we courageous enough to ask for honest feedback from our spouse and kids, and then take it seriously? Good self-assessment requires ongoing evaluation of our commitments at work and home. Too often we think "I'll spend some time with the kids tomorrow," or "I'll slow down next month." But when "tomorrow" comes we find we have lost our kids and become alienated from our spouse.

SUPPORT GROUPS FOR MENTAL HEALTH PROFESSIONALS

An excellent place to begin dealing with the difficulties of self-definition that have been a product of our upbringing, as well as our unmet needs for appreciation, is a professional support group. Groups can provide us with the opportunity to get to know ourselves as individuals and as individuals-with-others.

These groups must be structured to ensure trust and confidence. Frequently, this means finding a support group outside one's primary work setting. In some of the clergy support groups we have run, several clergy have commented on the importance of having a safe group outside of their own church, and even denomination, so that they can open up and talk about their feelings without fear that their words will get back to their bishop or denominational executive. The same need for confidentiality and anonymity applies to psychotherapists. Exploring issues around countertransference, personal struggles, and difficult clients apart from one's work setting is an invaluable experience. Professionals working in a mental health agency may wish to talk not only about problems with clients, but also about agency structures, bureaucracy, and administrative concerns. Safety and confidentiality are essential in this regard. The ideal situation may be to meet with groups of people from a variety of agencies doing roughly similar kinds of work. It is ideal because this configuration combines personal anonymity with professional familiarity, and it allows a cross-fertilization of ideas. Meeting with other professionals from other settings but with similar interests and problems may be optimal.

Within the support group it is useful to focus on parallels between the family of origin and work systems. For example, Maria was part of a support group comprised of two social workers, two psychologists, and a family therapist. They agreed in their initial contract to exchange genograms with each other, as a way of becoming better acquainted with each other's family of origin issues as they interacted with current work issues. As Maria talked about how she was feeling more and more tired of her administrative responsibilities in the large mental health setting in which she worked, several people in her group reminded her of how overresponsible she had been in her family of origin. Maria said it felt like she had become a parent to a group of irresponsible children in her present job, much as she had felt growing up feeling responsible for her own parents. She talked on several occasions about how she knew she should hold her coworkers accountable and delegate more responsibility, but deep down she was afraid that if she did they would just mess things up anyway, as her parents had done. The group was able to help her explore ways of giving up some of her responsibilities by appropriate delegation of some of her responsibilities to colleagues, and continued to support her as she experienced much anxiety in the process.

The group becomes a place not only for intellectual exploration of family of origin and work patterns, but also for practice in being vulnerable and open. This can be a crucial step in preventing burnout. Staying in touch with one's vulnerable self by sharing it in a supportive group context is a helpful antidote to getting caught up in the unconscious grandiosity that comes from trying to be too helpful. Cheryl, for example, finally took a risk in her support group and acknowledged that she was fearful of her coworkers' not liking her and so constantly did more than her share in hopes of pleasing people. She was surprised and relieved to find that others in the support group acknowledged feeling the same way. Group members were then able to focus on how often their overworking was a way to ensure that people liked them and to start dealing more appropriately with the issue. After talking about her own experience, and hearing similar stories from others, Cheryl began to realize that the approval she might have gotten for doing more than her share was only for the work she did, not for herself.

By providing a safe place for people to examine family of origin issues and get in touch with their vulnerability, support groups encourage healthier self-definition. For instance, Jeremy, the director of a family counseling center, told his support group how tired he was feeling. Weighed down by a high caseload of multiproblem families and children who had been sexually abused, problems dealing with managed care companies, pressure to do fund raising, and difficulty in delegating tasks, he was feeling overwhelmed. In spite of this he continued to take on more responsibility by chairing an important committee for his professional organization, as well as serving on the board of directors of another not-for-profit organization. He reported that each time he was asked to take on another job, he wanted to say no but inevitably wound up saying yes. On the few occasions when he contemplated saying no, he felt very anxious—one sign that an activity is driven and compulsive. At the same time his wife was complaining that she felt no support from Jeremy, leaving her lonely and distant.

The support group recognized how Jeremy's overfunctioning in his family of origin was continuing in his work environment. Jeremy felt safe enough to admit to the group that he knew he was driven by his sense of inadequacy and was becoming too dependent on the gratification he was receiving from his work. The group was able to help Jeremy take practical steps to set boundaries, such as resigning from one of his time-consuming committees and taking some risks in delegating work and decision-making. One of the group members suggested that Jeremy find an administrative mentor, to talk with periodically about how to delegate more appropriately. While this by no means solved Jeremy's problems, it was at least a beginning. The nurturing and safety of the support group members enabled Jeremy to trust enough to share some of his vulnerable self. This created a climate for devising and implementing practical strategies.

Unfortunately, there is one rather obvious problem with support groups. How does one find one? There are not a great many support groups to choose from. While some progressive agencies help professionals join an ongoing support group, most do very little in this regard. This leaves basically two options: Professionals can start their own groups, or they can look to their professional organizations for help. More than likely, most professionals will have to start their own groups, perhaps initially meeting informally a couple times a month with several trusted colleagues. While this will take some effort, in the long run it will be worth it. Several possibilities exist for starting a group. You could start a group with colleagues from your own agency as long as no one in the group had administrative responsibility for others in the group. Another possibility would be to sponsor a lecture or workshop on burnout and use this meeting as a setting for inviting people to join a support group. Or advertise in one of the trade journals or professional meeting places where interested parties might come. Or finally, call around to some of your friends or colleagues from other agencies and invite them to talk over coffee about the possibilities of starting a support group. Obviously, all of this involves effort and risk, but the long-term payoff in terms of prevention could be enormous.

In starting a support group several considerations are important. First, what is the focus of the group to be? Will the group be a general support group, a peer supervision group, or a group that is focused exclusively on how family of origin issues affect present work functioning? Second, the group must be structured as to be safe. This usually involves not being in a group with one's coworkers. Finally, once the group starts and the focus is clear, basic group contracting should be undertaken to determine how often the group will meet, for how long, how confidentiality will be dealt with, and other ground rules. The group must meet often enough to be cohesive but not so often as to be burdensome. Many find that meeting every two weeks for one and a half to two hours is optimal. The meeting could be a brown bag lunch, with the location rotating among the group members' offices. The group could meet over breakfast twice a month, or even over dinner. The key is to find a time that allows group members to make a commitment that they can keep and keeps the group from fizzling out.

Finally, in the formation of support groups, Pines's summary of the six functions of social support is helpful:

1. Listening (active listening, without giving advice or making judgments)
2. Technical support and appreciation (from a person who is an expert in the field and whose honesty can be trusted)
3. Technical challenge (from a person who is good enough at the job to be able to identify what could be improved and who can provide the challenge for our benefit and not at our expense)
4. Emotional challenge (from a person who can help us think rationally when we are too emotionally involved in a situation)
5. Emotional support (from a person who is on our side, no matter what)
6. Shared social reality (from a person who sees things the way we do and has similar values and priorities) (1993, p. 397)

Pines notes that a support group fulfilling at least three of these functions will help prevent burnout. Starting or joining a support group that is attentive to these items can be enormously helpful in the prevention of burnout.

EFFECTIVE SUPERVISION

Another key to prevention of burnout is receiving good supervision on a regular basis. While this may seem obvious, it is rare to find mental health professionals who are satisfied with the caliber of supervision they receive. Earlier we detailed some of the problems of agency-based supervision, including paradigm clashes (such as trying to provide psychodynamic therapy in an uncongenial setting, or to use a family systems approach in an agency whose supervisors work only with individuals) and conflicts between administrative supervision and clinical supervision. Obviously, if the supervisor has administrative responsibilities, then the clinical supervision will most likely not feel safe. How many people are going to reveal how stuck they feel with certain clients, or acknowledge that they are attracted to a client, to a supervisor who is then going to write their evaluation and has the power to fire them? Unfortunately, those therapists who do open up to their administrative superiors (often with such people's active encouragement) often find out later what a mistake this mixing of roles can turn out to be.

In addition to these obvious problems, most supervisors have little or no training in supervision, either in terms of theories of supervision or actual supervision of their supervision. Many professional organizations do not even have a designated category of approved supervisors specifically trained in the practice of supervision. (The American Association of Marriage and Family Therapists, the American Association of Pastoral Counselors, and the Association for Clinical Pastoral Education all certify supervisors.)

The odds of getting high quality supervision at work are slim. One way to secure effective supervision is to contract for supervision with a seasoned supervisor outside of the agency. This person should have no evaluative function and a personal psychotherapeutic paradigm that is congruent with the supervisee's. Outside supervision provides a safe context in which to work on specific learning goals, distinct from those of the agency, and to explore countertransference reactions or why one habitually gets stuck or overinvolved with certain types of clients. To many professionals paying for private supervision seems like a luxury. They may resent the idea of having to pay, or think that it's terribly expensive, or even resent their agency for not providing better supervision. One way to lower the cost of supervision is to form a supervision group of three to five professionals, who split the cost. The cost will be further reduced if the group meets only every two or three weeks or even once a month. In the end it costs far less than might be imagined, and the benefits in terms of growth and prevention of burnout far outweigh the cost.

Supervision can and should be a place where the learning goals of the supervisee are taken seriously. Too often agency-based supervision is of necessity focused on case management, including checking to see if case notes and files are in order and meet agency standards or if quality improvement standards are being satisfied. Exploration of the goals of the supervisee is not encouraged and frequently avoided altogether. In reality, one of the problems in the mental health field is that many of us are undertrained and feel inadequate with at least some of our cases. Good supervision increases our ability to work effectively and feel more self-confident and self-assured. In addition, when supervision is safe and focused on the theory and technique of the supervisee, the supervisory relationship becomes a selfobject relationship for the professional, which will enhance a sense of well-being and confidence. Unfortunately, while learning theory stresses that the learner should formulate and articulate goals, too often the supervisor's goals dominate. Learning goals are not met, and in worst case scenarios the supervisee feels abused.

Much of the literature on supervision discusses the stages of supervision (Liddle, Breunlin, & Schwartz, 1988; Stoltenberg & Delworth, 1987). Usually at least three supervisory stages are specified: early, middle, and late. In each of these stages different needs, expectations, and learning goals are apparent. Stoltenberg and Delworth (1987) are helpful in spelling this out in more detail. They assess trainees in terms of motivation, autonomy, and self and other awareness, as well as in terms of specific skills such as assessment, treatment planning, client conceptualization, and a number of other categories.

At each level of professional expertise different supervision interventions are called for. At level one, for example, trainees tend to be anxious and dependent on supervision. They need a good deal of structure and supervising support, as well as frequently needing to bolster an inadequate knowledge base. If the supervisor does not provide enough structure, without taking over the case, the supervisee will flounder and become more anxious, perhaps pushing him or her close to early disillusionment in the field. Stoltenberg and Delworth suggest that at this level beginning professionals prefer modeling, receiving positive feedback, structure, sharing counseling experiences, and suggestions of literature to be read (1987, p. 59).

Level-two supervisees are more assertive and need to begin developing their own style. At the same time, they are realizing that no theory has all the answers, and that client change seems elusive. While their skills have vastly improved, there is frequently discouragement that therapy does not work as they thought it would. The supervisor must now provide a different supervisory environment to accommodate the needs of this stage, which allows for growing autonomy, clarification of ambivalence, and less of a didactic focus. The supervisee's frustration may also be vented on the supervisor, who must be able to help work this through without becoming defensive or authoritative.

Professionals at level three are motivated and can carry out clinical responsibilities in a fairly autonomous way. They are largely aware of their strengths and weaknesses and know what they need from a supervisor. At this stage the supervisor can be more of a consultant, use more self-disclosure, and facilitate a more collaborative approach to supervision.

Whether one accepts Stoltenberg and Delworth's model or not, it raises important concerns about the stages of the supervisory process. Working with a supervisor who understands that supervisees have different needs, and who can create a supervisory environment congruent both with the developmental stage of the professional coming for supervision, and with the unique learning goals of the supervisee, can be a wonderful preventive measure against burnout. The sensitive supervisor is aware of these issues and creates a learning environment where appropriate learning goals can be formulated and addressed. Moreover, when supervision is perceived as safe and nurturing, it becomes a safe place to process countertransference reactions. When transference and countertransference issues are openly and honestly discussed, inappropriate involvement with clients can be prevented. Professionals who are aware of their own countertransference reactions are less likely to use clients to meet archaic selfobject needs. A good supervisor can be very useful in helping a therapist monitor these transference and countertransference reactions.

Another productive form of supervision is provided by peer supervision groups, where a group of professionals meet together regularly to review cases and provide mutual supervision in an informal context. These supervision groups can be extremely helpful and growth-producing. Peer supervision groups can take several forms. One involves professionals meeting regularly to review and discuss video and audiotapes of each other's sessions, in order to improve their psychotherapeutic techniques. Other groups focus on understanding and utilizing countertransference in work with clients. Still others become study groups; while less personal, these can be a helpful and focused way to learn theory and technique and gain perspective on one's day-to-day work.

When they have been meeting regularly over time, these groups often can become a safe forum not only for the processing of difficult cases but also for monitoring and review of transference and countertransference material. Within a safe support group, the potential exists for mental health professionals to explore their vulnerable selves, as well as get creative input from colleagues. These groups are only helpful when they meet regularly and consistently and when trust builds among the group members. When meetings are allowed to become irregular, or when one person's needs are allowed to dominate the discussion, the group can stop working. A certain structure, such as a rotation schedule that guarantees each person a turn at presenting material, is essential.

Both good one-on-one supervision and a healthy peer supervision group contribute to the prevention of burnout. In these contexts mental health professionals experience support that will aid in the development of self esteem, even while they stay in touch with the vulnerable self. As long as adult learning goals are addressed, supervision is a safe context in which to grow professionally and not become stagnant, as well as to deal with transference and countertransference issues.

BALANCING LOVE AND WORK AND PLAY

A final aspect of prevention is finding balance in one's life. We have deliberately mentioned this last for a couple of reasons. First, it is frequently overused as advice, resulting in very little change or prevention. Second, unless one attends to family of origin themes and how they influence one's professional life, and unless one attempts to better understand personal needs for admiration, it will be difficult to find balance.

Balance includes taking care of primary relationships, as well as finding time for one's physical, emotional, and spiritual needs. Sometimes this is fairly simple. For instance, one colleague found he could refresh himself by taking long lunches. When feeling worn out and exhausted, he would go to a restaurant for upwards of an hour, often with a book, and return relieved from stress. Sometimes he would do this with a friend, but this required more energy and was not as much of an indulgence, so he would usually go alone.

Another preventive is exercise, as long as it doesn't become a compulsion. Much like a hobby, exercise, like running or hiking, can be a positive resource and a source of satisfaction. Strenuous exercise can also be health-enhancing. The sports analogy is useful here. It is possible to be in vigorous training, such as for a marathon, without getting injured. One can work hard while maintaining vigilance to avoid psychological injury or burnout. An athlete in training for competition has to maintain a constant awareness of how to avoid injury. If we are going to be good—that is, effective—therapists, we have to remain healthy.

Staying healthy means also nurturing one's spiritual self. Who has not felt like a well which clients draw from—a well that is often in danger of going dry. The well must have water continuously flowing into it to keep this from happening. In that regard finding spiritual refreshment is essential. Taking an occasional afternoon to just sit, taking someone to a play, finding a place that encourages contemplation—an art gallery, park, or country setting—may be one source of refreshment. This can be found in attending weekly services at a place of worship. For others it may involve learning to meditate or pray or connect with what the late Protestant theologian Paul Tillich called the "ground of all being" (1952). Most recovery groups stress the need for a higher power, and perhaps that is also an important part of prevention and growth.

We have discovered in colleagues and in ourselves that lack of control over the type of work we do can be a source of stress. Unlike many private practitioners who don't see patients they don't like, counselors in public agencies are frequently faced with patients who don't come, don't listen, and don't pay. Mental health professionals working in public inpatient settings cannot avoid violence-prone involuntary patients. As one colleague put it, "Working in public mental health is like rearranging deck chairs on the Titanic." These types of agencies require more diligence in building balanced lives. However, in attempting to find balance, an additional obstacle may have to be overcome; this is known as adrenaline overarousal.

Though technically not an addiction, a form of hurry sickness develops whenever we are caught up in a lifestyle that is pressure-filled and demanding. If there is more to do than there is time to do it in; particularly if the work has some risk associated with it, adrenaline surges are inevitable. Revved-up feelings and a sense of power can be highly pleasurable. In fact, sustained activity may provide selfobject experience—a sense of vitalization. A frenetic lifestyle can be both a defense against and a cause of burnout. When the rush is over, the feeling of drop-off can be quite depressing.

For many, then, the avoidance of this lull becomes a preoccupation (thus, racquetball several times a week). To avoid feeling the letdown (which in many respects is similar to drug withdrawal), many therapists work at staying busy, filling off-hours and office lulls with hectic activity. Relaxation, really, is challenging hard work. In fact, to many successful professionals, relaxation is—or would be, if they did it—the hardest job of all.

Liz is a classic example. A highly respected psychiatrist, she has a psychiatric emergency service (crisis intervention unit) practice, two small children, and a supportive husband. She tries to balance work and recreation by regularly taking time off. She plans family trips to a lakeside family-owned cabin. But even during vacations, she feels a strong, inexplicable compulsion to do something. She has to do chores, wash the curtains, work or repair projects around the cabin, catch up on journal reading, cook gourmet meals—anything. Even when she tries to relax, she can't.

According to Archibald Hart, author of *Adrenaline and Stress*, it is not simply the young, super-energetic, type-A personality that is prone to adrenaline dependency. This subtle disorder takes many forms and imprisons all kinds of people. Even those who do not appear to be overstressed may be a boiling cauldron inside. A calm exterior may mask a racing mind and a constant search for excitement.

This becomes yet another area to be assessed in the interest of prevention. What are the signs to be looking for? The signs include always being in a hurry with never enough time; a constant need for stimulation and excitement; feeling fidgety, restless, and impatient during times of inactivity; and generally a time of depression following a very intense and busy time.

One of the dangers of this addiction to adrenaline is that

non-work activities, including recreation, can feed the addiction. If careers are busy and demanding, hobbies and activities may be chosen that follow suit. When work and play both become physically and emotionally taxing, the risk for hypertension and other stress-related disorders increases exponentially.

In addition to physiological damage, chronic intense activity is dangerous in other ways as well. When helping professionals run at full speed for years, they become vulnerable to "hitting the wall." The phrase "hitting the wall" is used by marathon runners to describe the experience, at about the 20-mile mark, where the runner feels like he or she cannot go another step. They feel as if they have completely run out of fuel. When this happens to professionals it is generally a very frightening experience, from which it may take months or years to recover.

It is important for helping professionals to be able to assess overdependence on adrenaline, as well as to know what steps can be taken to minimize the dependence. Some steps might include learning to recognize when you are overdoing it, and perhaps attempting to slow down. It may involve scheduling periods of inactivity, and perhaps even setting aside a day to do nothing. Obviously, it also involves building adequate rest periods into our lives, and developing healthy, relaxing habits. This is easier said than done.

Tony, a psychologist we interviewed, shared with us that he had had three sports-related injuries in the last year, necessitating long recovery times. His position as supervising psychologist is demanding. Between running fifty miles a week in preparation for marathons and excessive weight training, his body has begun to break down, with several major injuries over the last year. He says he ought to know better, but reports getting "antsy" and irritable when he does not work out. He says he is addicted to the "running high," but jokes that at least it is a positive addiction. He, unfortunately, illustrates the difficulty of slowing down, and is a prime candidate for burnout.

SUMMARY

When looking at the issue of prevention, many writers suggest that the work system should provide an environment that is conducive to growth, and so help professionals avoid burnout. Obviously, much could be written about the work system's potential contributions to the prevention of burnout. However, the issue we are most concerned about is how mental health professionals can define themselves appropriately within these systems so as to avoid the burnout that comes from counterproductive feedback loops.

Being part of a support group that works on family of origin issues, differentiation of self, and healthy narcissism can be a very important part of prevention. Securing good supervision outside of one's agency or being part of a peer supervision group can also be extremely helpful in maintaining professional growth, aiding in appropriate self-definition, and sorting out complex countertransference reactions. In addition, finding ways to balance love and work, as well as periodically expanding and enhancing your skills and sense of competence, through travel, conventions, workshops, reading, supervision, and personal therapy, are helpful. Learning to exchange ideas with colleagues instead of getting stuck in the rut of solitary activity also helps. Finally, when you have done a thorough self-assessment, part of prevention may involve choosing to leave a position that does not permit growth, and then looking for a work setting that offers the best likelihood for using one's talents and fulfilling one's aspirations.

6

WOUNDED HEALERS OR GRANDIOSE SAVIORS: THE TREATMENT OF BURNOUT

Prevention strategies are designed to keep professionals from experiencing the emotional agony of burnout; all too often, however, the problem isn't identified until it's too late for prevention. By the time most people begin to recognize the physical, emotional, and spiritual symptoms of burnout, the problem is already well advanced. At this point, although they are urgently in need of the type of help they provide to others, emotionally depleted workers may not realize just how entrenched and deep the problem is.

The same factors that make early detection and prevention difficult, including the narcissistic gratifications of overwork and the fact that emotional depletion is an insidious process, also complicate the treatment of burnout. Understanding treatment, from our integrated model, involves looking at diagnosis, treatment options, the phases of the treatment process as well as aspects and complications of that process, and finally, the desired outcome of treatment.

SELF DIAGNOSIS: THE STARTING POINT

How, then, is burnout to be detected before it becomes too late to reverse the process? The truth is that the symptoms of work exhaustion are frequently missed because it is easy to assume that any frustration or weariness we might feel derives simply from the special circumstances of our work alone, which by its very nature keeps us in one-way relationships. Since it is human nature to first look outside ourselves for the causes of our lack of success or satisfaction, we may fail to make the diagnosis of burnout. If we were to assume first that burnout was due just to overwork—too many hours on the job—we would probably be wrong. On the other hand, we would be in error to think of this diagnosis only in terms of the medical model (which, like it or not, most of us carry around in our heads), according to which we assume that problems must be located in the individual. We are well aware that a disease model is inadequate for understanding a syndrome that has significant psychosocial determinants. The burned-out helper is depressed; something *is* wrong with him. However, burnout involves both individual and circumstantial factors; something about the interaction of the person and his or her work environment is leading to overload. The real problem exists in the nature of the work and in the fact that many people seek narcissistic gratification from a job that turns out to be (and always was) basically selfless.

Noted diagnostician John Wing has pointed out that one of the key tests for the value of a diagnosis is whether it results in improved treatment:

> To put forward a diagnosis is, first of all, to recognize a condition, and then to put forward a theory about it. Theories are meant to be tested. The most obvious test is whether applying a theory is helpful to the patient. Does it accurately predict a form of treatment that reduces disability without leading to harmful side effects? (1977, p. 87)

The World Health Organization has included Burnout as a V code diagnosis in ICD-10 under the section entitled, "Supplementary Classification of Factors Influencing Health Status and Contact with Health Services." Although criteria are not delineated for making the diagnosis, this new category recognizes the usefulness of this designation. This revision represents an advance over the two closest entries in ICD-9: "Adverse effects of work environment" and "other occupational circumstances or maladjustment," which included career choice problems and dissatisfaction with employment. Unfortunately, sufficient empirical research is lacking to elevate Burnout to V code status in DSM-IV, which retains V62.2 Occupational Problem. As in ICD-9, examples include job dissatisfaction and uncertainty about career choice. The absence of burnout as a diagnosis in DSM-IV unfortunately forces a choice between occupational problem and some other official diagnosis implying greater dysfunction in order to merit attention. In other words, it may be underdiagnosed if not missed altogether or overdiagnosed based on the categories available in DSM-IV.

Research findings (Freudenberger, 1974) clearly indicate that those who are dedicated, idealistic, and highly committed are at risk for burnout. Yet don't most of us in the helping professions think of ourselves in these terms? Obviously, then, these characteristics alone are not sufficient to predict burnout. Additional pressures are necessary.

What are some of the telltale signs? Feelings of depletion, irritability, poor sleep, and physical problems, such as headaches or gastrointestinal disturbances, lead the list. Other symptoms include loss of enthusiasm, boredom, indecision, lack of concentration (easy distractibility), and withdrawal from coworkers. Negative attitudes towards work, other people, and life in general are common. Feeling inadequate or omnipotent are characteristic. These characteristics include physiological, psychological, and vocational aspects. Those who tend towards the omnipotent pole of adaptation are unfortunately the least likely to make a self-diagnosis, unless a crisis occurs as a result of poor judgment based on an exaggerated sense of personal power. Unfortunately, when diagnosis follows a crisis, burnout has already reached serious proportions.

Though we may never or only reluctantly admit that we are burned-out, perhaps it is possible to consider, even accept, when we are in the process of burning out. We may be able to learn from experience if we've had previous episodes of exhaustion and near collapse. If we're able to appreciate the early signs and symptoms of occupational overload, we'll be able to stamp out the flickering flames after the kindling has been lit.

OPTIONS FOR TREATMENT

Once burnout has been assessed or diagnosed, what are the options for treatment? Basically there are four: (1) self-help, (2) therapy or support groups, (3) individual psychotherapy, and (4) inpatient treatment.

Self-help

Options include attempting to find out the extent of burnout that others in the organization are experiencing. Uncovering the deleterious operational and structural characteristics in the work structure may go a long way toward treatment of the underlying causes. As one joins with coworkers and attempts to change the structural dynamics of the work environment, some relief from the early stages of burnout might occur. This relief may come as the result of actually changing the structure or from a renewed sense of collegiality in joining with coworkers to attack the problem. What can people do collectively? They can bargain to modify or reduce caseloads, urge or propose modifications in burdensome chart procedures, identify and speak to or complain about unhelpful supervisors, plan some form of regular meetings that will make the work more interesting, and initiate a multitude of other strategies.

Many mental health clinics and agencies are organized in rigid hierarchies, with one or two levels of management and line staff. A typical situation is one in which a person in a supervisory capacity reports to a director and in turn is responsible for leading a team. Such persons often feel under much pressure to know what to do and always come up with the right decision. Certain self-initiated strategies can help. As a team leader you can shift to a more democratic style. Instead of putting pressure on oneself to come up with answers, ask the group for their ideas. Let other group members react. Although the final decision and authority (and pressure) rests with the team leader, this process spreads the load and increases input. A second idea is to open up with the director, if such person shows him or herself to be supportive and helpful. However, if not, it's best to realize that this may not be the person to open up to about problems you're having. Instead, find someone else. Additionally, many professionals find it enormously helpful to meet on some regular basis with peers on the same level. This may require some ingenuity to set up sessions with other team leaders, supervisors, clinic directors, or middle-level managers.

Other self-help options include attempting to vary one's activities by changing positions within an organization, looking for opportunities for taking a study leave or brief sabbatical, and contracting to do some additional work with an outside supervisor or even an externship at a postgraduate institution. These growth opportunities may revitalize tired professionals and create a temporary sense of relief. It is doubtful, however, that they will resolve the underlying causes of burnout.

Support Groups

As with prevention, another treatment option is to find or organize a support group. If part of what is operating within professionals prone to burnout is a desperate need for mirroring and affirmation, which inevitably tends to be frustrated, then support groups can provide the opportunity to better understand motivations and to move towards greater self-integration. When there is acceptance, validation, and understanding, you will be more inclined to explore and express yourself, to become aware of and integrate hitherto unacceptable aspects of yourself, and to relate more deeply and effectively to others.

According to Yalom (1985), self-esteem is enhanced by membership in a cohesive group. In our experience with clergy support groups, as well as with individual clergy in therapy groups, the group commonly evaluates the individual more highly than he or she evaluates himself or herself. The new member, in a state of dissonance, will try to resolve the discrepancy. A common ploy is to lower the group's opinion by revealing personal inadequacies. Usually this effort has the paradoxical effect of raising the group's esteem and acceptance of the new member even more, since disclosure of inadequacies is a cherished group norm (Yalom, 1985).

Occasionally, in heterogeneous groups we have found that the group evaluates the member who is a mental health professional *less* highly than he or she evaluates himself or herself. Some of the factors that may account for this include members' need to see a mental health professional as immune to emotional problems, negative experience with previous therapy, stereotypes of therapist aloofness and arrogance, and a reaction formation against envy and idealization. The anticipation of such attitudes is often a deterrent to group membership. The mental health professional who is a patient will sometimes rationalize that the group is artificial or composed of highly disturbed individuals and compare it to some other reference group (i.e., professionals) that might evaluate him or her differently. This anxiety often leads to termination from group therapy.

When group therapy is successful the individual has felt sufficiently accepted and has been able to raise his or her public esteem by changing those traits and attitudes criticized in the group. Thus, for example, Kathy felt more accepted and appreciated after she learned to be a more attentive listener and refrained from prematurely giving advice and exhibiting a know-it-all attitude. According to Yalom, this method of resolution is more likely if the individual is attracted to the group and if the discrepancy between the low public esteem and higher self-esteem is not too great. Too much arrogance and superiority are not conducive to membership appeal or popularity.

While there are a great many self-help measures that can be talked about, including those discussed in the previous chapter, more often than not self-help measures are ineffective when one has reached the later stages of burnout. It is time to seek professional help.

Psychotherapy

Therapists who recognize their own burnout as beyond self-help measures ordinarily seek individual psychotherapy in order to reduce public exposure and tarnish to their reputation. Also, since many mental health professionals postpone getting help until they are in an advanced stage of burnout, often characterized by serious symptomatology, individual therapy is often required in the initial stages in order to achieve stabilization. Group approaches become useful and desirable as a second phase of the rehabilitative process and serve a healthy maintenance function. Those more foresighted in early stages of burnout are generally receptive to entering a homogeneous peer group for ongoing support, catharsis, and self-examination.

Many therapists are too ashamed to seek out a support group. To admit having lost the inner meaning of their own message would be a confession of failure to live up to the principles for which they stand. It would mean exposing their failure to practice what they preach. Often, psychotherapists suffer from the occupational hazard of thinking they are immune from emotional ills and assume they'll be able to copc with stress. They may forget that they have wounds and are always in need of healing themselves. Yet, the experience of their own helplessness often opens them to the discovery of some new possibility; they start to find an inner source of self-worth that is more basic than trying to be a perfect God-like person who blesses and saves everybody else.

While psychotherapy is the treatment of choice for these burned-out professionals, the process is not simple. Below we discuss the stages and complications of such treatment.

Just as in most psychotherapy, the treatment of burnout usually moves through three stages; an early stage, a middle stage, and a resolution and termination stage. (Also like most forms of psychotherapy, not every case need progress through all three stages; some cases resolve quickly in the first stage.) However, the nature of these stages differs from most psychotherapy.

In stage one the therapist must take a directive stance with the burned-out professional. Most likely the burned-out professional is looking for some straightforward help in dealing with a very painful problem. The therapist should begin by working actively with the burned-out professional to devise some very concrete problem-solving activities. These activities may not succeed, but they may provide some relief, as well as additional assessment information, and establish a contract for the second stage of treatment.

During this first stage, the therapeutic task is to help the professional get some objective perspective on the system. That is, the professional must be helped to step back from the work situation and nonreactively observe the system and his/her role in the system from some distance. Ideally, she will identify her interactional pattern within the system and then problem-solve around how she can change her stance to move towards more balance.

Changing oneself in the system is easier said than done. Even when we recognize the pain of our current situation and resolve to modify our position in a work or family system, we are likely to find ourselves sucked right back into our previous role in short order. It is this frustration that launches treatment into a second phase. If the therapist continues to urge the professional to change his/her interactional position in the work organization, and the professional is repeatedly failing, the therapist is simply compounding the problem. This is the time to ask why changing one's mode of operation is so difficult. Usually that initiates family of origin exploration. Not surprisingly, professionals frequently find to their consternation that they are replaying old roles in new systems. Efforts to change one's patterns of behavior run contrary to old patterns of family loyalty and ways of relating. *Sometimes* simply recognizing that you are replaying old family conflicts at work can free you from following the old script; often, however, added to the maddening recognition that you are acting like your parents or your own teenage selves is the even more maddening discovery that you can't seem to stop yourself from doing so.

Once you begin to recognize some of the ways you are replaying old family scripts, you might consider returning home (to the source of these conflicts) and rewriting your part. Notice what your parents say or do that makes you reactive. Notice the old roles you begin to slip into. *Notice*, don't rush to change. Later, when you try to change things, remember that you can't change other people, only yourself in relationship to them.

The two most important changes you can make in your family are removing yourself as much as possible from triangles and learning to tone down your tendency to react emotionally to your parents' provocations. Removing yourself from triangles is simple, and sometimes almost simply impossible. But try. Whenever one person complains to you about another, or whenever you hear a story in which one person is a villain and the other a victim, you are being invited to participate in a triangle. When your mother complains to you about your father, suggest that she talk to him. Then suggest that you don't want to hear it. When your father does what he does that drives you crazy, try not to fall back into fight or flight. Humor him. Thank him for ignoring you. Recognize his point of view, then calmly state your own. Don't argue, and don't cave in. Let your family members be themselves (you might as well, they will be anyway), but be yourself.

Therapy at this level stirs deep feelings, old wounds, and long-standing insecurities. The therapist is now much better able through staying empathically attuned to the pain of the burned-out professional to see many of the deeper underlying issues shaped in interaction with the family of origin in the early years of life. Nouwen (1972) reminds us that the healer's task is not to take away pain, but rather to deepen the pain to a level where it can be shared. Working at this level touches several aspects of the treatment process, which are discussed below under "Complications in the Treatment of Burnout."

In the third and final stage the professional is challenged to apply the gains of therapy in some concrete ways involving better self-definition at work. In this final stage of treatment, two major outcomes are desired: First, it is hoped that, now that some significant issues have been worked through, the professional is more cohesive and more differentiated, such that he or she can better define a self to the work system, thereby preventing future burnout. Second, it is hoped that through psychotherapy the burned-out professional can embrace the image of the wounded healer, that is, to see oneself not only as a helper but also as one who needs to be helped. Both of these outcomes can be enhanced by the addition of group therapy during the third phase of treatment. But before we explore various aspects of the treatment process, let us deal briefly with the treatment option of hospitalization.

Inpatient Treatment

Advanced burnout may achieve the status of illness, e.g., clinical depression, or contribute to the exacerbation of another illness, e.g., heart attack, duodenal ulcer disease, ulcerative colitis, or irritable bowel syndrome (spastic colitis). Any of these medical conditions could result in hospitalization. In these cases, the hospital admission would not be for the treatment of burnout per se; however, adequate biopsychosocial inquiry or possible psychiatric consultation might lead to the recognition of burnout as a background phenomenon worthy of special care and treatment.

The despair and depletion of burnout may progress to clinical depression or anxiety disorder, which if serious enough, may require inpatient psychiatric treatment. As always, hospitalization must be considered in cases of suicidal behavior.

COMPLICATIONS IN THE TREATMENT OF BURNOUT

The Shame of Needing Treatment

As a result of early repetitive selfobject failure, the self experiences shame in the presence of need itself. In other words, when one is unable to attain alone the ideal of power (sustained professional effectiveness) or self-soothing and must look instead to another to provide such functions (a therapist, for example), one frequently feels ashamed of passivity, weakness, and need. Shame as an affective experience can best be appreciated as a reflection of passive failure, defeat, or depletion (burnout) (Morrison, 1989, p. 82). Shame is a particular problem in treatment of burned-out psychotherapists because they feel that they have failed in the arena where they are most proud. In addition, as therapists begin to realize that their "selfless devotion" to helping is in part a means of propping themselves up by being good and kind enough to earn other people's admiration and appreciation, they are almost always embarrassed. We believe that it is extremely important to recognize that burnout is inherently shame-provoking, since it is so often associated with feelings of ineffectiveness and failure. Recognizing the shame of needing treatment in the burned-out mental health professional creates the possibility of addressing it appropriately.

The Expression of Personal Dynamics in Overwork

While overwork results in some serious personal problems, often personal problems cause the overwork. If we assume that overwork causes burnout, we will suggest a solution that involves working less. Unfortunately, people too often lie to themselves and their families and say that circumstances won't allow them to cut back. We need to remember that we can seldom cut back on compulsive activity without experiencing tremendous anxiety. Also, working less runs up against the deeper longing to be loved, appreciated, and taken seriously; desires and needs that many helpers never learned to satisfy in more direct ways. These desires and needs will have to be addressed in order for treatment to be productive.

The Need to Overcome Shame Through Acceptance of the Grandiose Self While Avoiding Lowering Overly Strong Ideals

Initially, Kohut (1971) understood shame as resulting from the power of the grandiose ambitions. Whenever the self is overwhelmed with grandiosity, this will inevitably result in a feeling of failure and shame. The ambitious or success-driven therapist in pursuit of external success (promotion, tenure, financial reward) will respond to any failure with shame. Treatment of shame-prone patients such as wearied mental health professionals requires the therapist's acceptance and confirmation of the patient's grandiose self. Therapists who encounter shame are often tempted to offer reassurance, telling patients that they have nothing to be ashamed of. Actually, this reassurance isn't very reassuring, for it does little more than tell patients that they shouldn't feel what they feel. Archaic grandiosity and shame-provoking exhibitionism, if empathically accepted, will eventually become transformed into self-esteem and pleasure in success. Kohut discovered, and we agree, that, "progress in the analysis of shame-prone people is usually not achieved on the basis of trying to diminish the power of overly strong ideals" (1978, p. 70).

According to Morrison (1989, pp. 80–81), shame is the hallmark of the defeated self in a state of depletion, the self that has fallen short of goals. This would be true whether the despair reflected the subjective experience of frustrated grandiose ambitions, failed attempts to compensate for unrealized ambitions, or unmet yearnings to attain ideals. The discovery, examination, and working-through of shame by the patient, with the realization that he or she can be accepted as is, make successful treatment possible. Here therapists who, through vicarious introspection of their own personal failure to achieve goals and to realize ambitions and ideals, have recognized their own narcissistic grandiosity, will be at an advantage. In short, therapists must be willing to face and acknowledge their own shame and the pain that accompanies it.

Work as the Cleanest Addiction

Seeking solace and love through work may be the cleanest addiction we have. Often the yearnings that motivate people to choose careers in the health profession also propel them to put all of their emotional energy into work that promises but does not deliver the love they need.

According to Lichtenberg (1991), selfobject experiences can derive from ideas or beliefs that heighten self-esteem. Religion, for example, promises an enduringly available, protective deity. A psychologist's belief that she is a gifted therapist can be invoked whenever needed.

Therapists may come to rely on a conscious belief or an unconscious fantasy system as a source of selfobject experience to relieve distress and raise self-esteem. This is not in itself pathological, although some beliefs and fantasies and their enactment may be maladaptive. For instance, the illusion of omnipotence may have pathologic consequences if the individual does not recognize that it is serving as a means to create an affect state of invigoration or cohesion that might otherwise be lacking. Rescue fantasies, for example, are not entirely dysfunctional because the person gains professional fulfillment doing effective work; trouble arises when the individual does not recognize that he/she uses the fantasy and attendant behavior as a means to relieve unrecognized distress from a variety of sources.

As long as the helping professional's primary motivation is to preserve the fantasy of omnipotent helpfulness and resist every effort to create doubt about its validity, little attention can be given to the actual sources of distress. More importantly, the addiction to the fantasy will distort all of his/her relationships, especially those with patients. Any threat to dislodge the belief or illusion or fantasy that has become the source of vitality and self-esteem will bring forth vigorous defensive maneuvers. Burned-out professionals may be exhausted by the efforts to maintain fantasies of omnipotence and all the consequent activity; to recreate consistently selfobject experiences, however brief and vulnerable; to avoid confrontation of deeper needs and desires; and to defend against the onslaughts of reality threatening to puncture the fantasy. It's hard to be God! Yet, a strong desire for sustainable selfobject experiences from more ordinary sources persists alongside the addictive search for triggers recognized to be maladaptive (Lichtenberg, 1991). The world of work provides a slippery slope into faulty functioning because it is generally so accepted as a domain of healthy and legitimate life satisfaction, one of the "ordinary sources" of mature selfobject experience (therefore, the cleanest addiction). Confronting the addiction while supporting healthy selfobject functioning requires empathy, tact, and a delicate sense of timing on the part of the therapist.

Perpetuation of a Reverse Selfobject Experience

We have come to appreciate the influence of forces deriving from the family of origin. Earlier we discussed how much overfunctioning stems from efforts to hold onto a pattern of behavior that was heavily rewarded in childhood, such as a reverse selfobject experience (Lee, 1988). The child may have been an overly important source of stimulation or support for a parent (thus, in reverse) and now, as an adult, continues to provide a self-evoking or self-sustaining function for others. The repetition of experiences of an abusive or exploitive nature (allowing the self to be used again) may have a strong organizing effect because of the intensity of the experience. Untiring efforts to please, do a good job, and always strive to be better may have been so ingrained in us as children that we carry these expectations over into our adult lives. Because these demands are taken for granted, it becomes critical to treatment to anticipate and interpret them in the transference. Many therapists who become patients try very hard to be "good," e.g., compliant, in therapy, even though we might expect them to know better.

THE IMAGE OF THE WOUNDED HEALER

Doing therapy with therapists is facilitated by consideration of the archetype of the wounded healer (Knight, 1986, pp. 34–49). The mythological image of Asklepios proclaims that the patient has a healer within and that the healer has a patient within (Guggenbuhl-Craig, 1971). Carl Jung, in interpreting the Greek myth of the wounded healer, emphasized that "only the wounded doctor can heal, whether that doctor be physician or priest" (1951, p. 116).

Many mental health professionals with narcissistic vulnerabilities and proneness to burnout give the impression that they are immune to weakness, illness, and wounds, and that their patients live in a completely different world. The healers then develop into therapists-without-wounds and can no longer release the inner healing factor in their patients or themselves. Moreover, their lack of effectiveness contributes to feelings of inadequacy and inferiority, facilitating the process of burnout.

According to James Knight, psychiatrist and minister, " . . . only the one who is open, sensitive, and *personally* knowledgeable about pain and suffering can participate in healing. One's own hurt, one's sensitive openness to the patient, gives the measure of one's power to heal" (1986, p. 34).

> Asklepios, the son of the god Apollo and the mortal woman Koronis, was wounded before birth. Koronis had been unfaithful to Apollo and was shot during her pregnancy by Apollo's sister Artemis, at the instigation of Apollo. While Koronis was on the funeral pyre, Apollo snatched his son Asklepios from her womb, saved him from the flames, and gave him to the healer Chiron to raise and instruct in the art of healing. The myth describes Asklepios' entry into the world as a miraculous birth in death. Chiron, to whom Asklepios was entrusted, was half human and half divine, and afflicted with an incurable wound by the poisoned arrows of Hercules. Thus, Chiron, a healer who needed healing himself, passed on to Asklepios the art of healing, the capacity to be at home in the darkness of suffering and there to find seeds of light and recovery. (pp. 34–35)

In the Asklepian tradition of healing, a paradox is at the heart of the mystery: The healer heals but at the same time the healer remains wounded. No one is without wounds, to be sure, but the underlying principle of the mystery relates to the true healer's inner awareness of a wound.

This is another way of saying that therapy requires empathy or vicarious introspection. Following Groesbeck (1975), both therapist and patient must experience the health-sickness polarity if the patient is to be freed and healed. The true healer does not stand outside of the healing experience as a disinterested observer; instead he or she must be ready to have his or her own wounds activated and reactivated (yet contained within). He/she works with a deep and abiding awareness of remaining forever a patient as well as a healer.

The healer takes the wounds of vulnerability and pain into the encounter and is able to remain in the presence of suffering patients who show the healer the intimacy of their hurts. The wounded healer is thus seen not just as a helper but as one who can be helped. Up to a point, this is a legitimate benefit of being a professional helper. The wounded healer enters the encounter as one who not only gives but also receives. Often, the highest form of giving is receiving, a letting in, a letting it happen. When patients sense that they can give something, that they can be helpful, the scene changes. Patients want to get well, but they do not want to be forced into being dependent on therapists who are active, controlling agents. Patients themselves want to be active participants in the healing endeavor. When patients have an impact on their therapist, such as correcting the therapist or giving advice and counsel to the therapist, the pleasure of being effective heightens self-esteem and advances the healing process. We recommend that therapists remain aware of the therapeutic power of being open to influence, without manipulating the therapy to artificially create these types of transactions. Actively seeking advice from a patient would probably be a boundary transgression.

Possibly the greatest message in the wounded-healer concept is that those in the healing and helping professions see themselves not only as helpers but also as persons who need to be helped. This is why we recommend consideration of this concept for therapists suffering from burnout and for those offering help and healing to these colleagues. Therapists treating healers who are burning out need to enter the healing encounter with an openness to receive. This means having an expectation that this treatment relationship will offer something personal that will be meaningful and significant. We can expect to become better psychotherapists and perhaps better human beings. This openness, this sensitivity, even an awareness of brokenness and mortality, set the stage for healing to flow back and forth between patient and healer. One cannot enter this healing arena as a healer, however, unless one's wounds are recognized and accepted. This must be the goal in any treatment of burnout for the therapist as well as therapist-patient. Does not the Biblical adage "physician, heal thyself" tell us this? The doctor is not separated from the patient, for the doctor, too, is in search of healing.

As Henri Nouwen points out in *The Wounded Healer*, the theme of the wounded healer implies that all healing has its source in the vulnerability of both the healer and the person to be healed. The aim of the healer is not so much to remove the pain of life as to interpret it. The evidence in the healer of woundedness or pain and of the transcendence or constructive endurance of it help to heal the patient.

Members of Alcoholics Anonymous cannot and will not permit themselves to forget their brokenness and vulnerability. Their wounds are acknowledged, accepted, and kept visible. The capacity of one alcoholic to empathize with another is still a recognized asset "building a transmission line" to him. The apparent (or presumable) effectiveness of AA's members in the care and treatment of their fellow alcoholics is one of the great success stories of our time, and graphically illustrates the power of wounds, when used creatively, to lighten the burden of pain and suffering. AA offers lifelong emotional support to those who explicitly acknowledge their problem and admit their helplessness to face life's stresses and temptations to regression alone.

Think of psychiatrist Harry Stack Sullivan, an isolated and lonely man, personally acquainted with mental illness. At the Sheppard and Enoch Pratt Hospital in Maryland he found himself truly at home in treating "untreatable" schizophrenic patients. Scarred by wounds of loneliness, Sullivan sensed that the lonely ones on the psychiatric wards, the withdrawn psychotic patients, were suffering from an illness the inner landscape of which he knew. Healing for Sullivan depended "on the doctor's and patient's shared humanness and mutual respect for the ambiguity and complexity inherent in human existence" (Knight, 1986, p. 44).

When John Wesley, Oxford professor, preacher, and founder of the Methodist Church, was five years old, he was the last member of his large family rescued when their home burned down. Wesley, appearing at an upstairs window with the flames raging around him, was pulled from the burning house by a neighbor standing on the shoulders of another. This experience made a deep and lasting impression on him, for he often referred to himself as a brand plucked from the burning by God. Like Asklepios in the Greek myth, he was snatched from the fires. His life covered almost the entire eighteenth century, and the imprint of death upon his life was carried as an energizing wound, as he wrote hundreds of articles and books, working with thousands of people from the slums of London to the Oglethorpe Colony in Georgia. Throughout his tumultuous life he was a healer with wounds. He never saw himself beyond the need for healing (Heitzenrater, 1984).

Anton T. Boisen (1954), theologian and father of the clinical pastoral training movement, has described his descent into the depths of psychotic illness and his arduous journey back to health. Buffeted into retreat from the world, he underwent a genuine spiritual rebirth. When he reestablished his bonds to the real world, he brought with him a message that moved his contemporaries to the depths. His unswerving belief that emotional illness could have positive use led him to become one of the first chaplains in a psychiatric hospital; to father clinical pastoral training in seminaries; and through research, teaching, writing, and patient care, to make an authentic and monumental contribution to the psychology of religion.

Healing comes through the wounded life. True healers, by virtue of coping with their own suffering and remaining fully aware of their own vulnerabilities, become pilgrims with others on the path to healing (Knight, 1986, p. 45). Accepting oneself as a wounded healer is not by itself enough to heal burnout. However, as we learn to integrate the more vulnerable parts of ourselves and accept our woundedness, we are much less likely to hold onto elaborate grandiose defenses. By embracing our own woundedness, as well as understanding how often work systems tend to replicate our family systems, we can learn to set boundaries and limits, say no, and take better care of ourselves at work. The ultimate goal of the treatment of burnout is to get professional helpers to accept themselves as wounded healers rather than grandiose saviors.

7

CASE STUDY: FEELING GOOD JUST FOR ME!

The following case illustrates the long-term psychotherapy of a counselor who was suffering from burnout. We have drawn from a chronological review of a twice weekly therapy that lasted over four years with William Grosch. The first stage of therapy was characterized by: (1) establishment of an empathic bond, which became the foundation for working toward better self-definition, and (2) the emergence of shame. In the middle stage the therapist fostered a healthy narcissism (a normal grandiose self), while the patient defended against excessive unmodified narcissism (repressed unfullfilled archaic narcissistic demands). The final termination stage lasted about six months.

PRESENTATION

Ellen, a 28-year-old social worker, arrived for her first appointment dressed casually in tan chinos and a brightly colored cotton shirt. She began the session describing her depression and unhappiness. Her work as a hospital-based social worker was becoming unmanageable; in fact, for the past several months she had dreaded going to work. Her burnout was complicated by a relationship with a married male coworker that had become sexual, as well as by problems with a new supervisor whom Ellen regarded as intrusive.

Ellen presented as bright, with good insight. She stated that she was confused about whether she was depressed, burned out, or just dealing with a problematic relationship. She joked in the first session about whether she should even be in therapy and talked about the many people who seemed to need therapy much more than she did. She felt almost guilty about taking their spot.

HISTORY

Ellen was the third child of four born to a psychologist father and mother who was a legal secretary. When asked about her family, she was guarded and talked about wanting to be emotionally independent from them while at the same time wanting to make them proud. She thinks some day she might move back to the midwest to be closer to them; at the same time she is afraid that her parents worry because she is not yet married.

She did very well academically in high school and placed near the top of her class in college with a degree in psychology. She dated sporadically but usually lost interest when relationships became too close. In her last year of graduate school, she ended what she thought was a serious relationship after discovering that the man was dating one of her friends.

After graduating from social work school, she worked for the department of social services. After struggling with a difficult supervisor for six months, she resigned and took a job in a medical center. For the past four years she has worked there in the patient and family counseling service. Six months before starting counseling, she was placed under the supervision of an older female supervisor, whom she saw as intrusive and overly critical. In addition, she has become involved with the married male coworker. She reported that she was becoming increasingly anxious about this relationship and what colleagues were thinking about it.

She noted that she had lost ten pounds in the last four months and was sleeping poorly. She felt out of control both with her supervisor and with the man she was involved with. At the same time she was beginning to lose confidence in her counseling ability. Due to a reorganization in her department, she felt overburdened with disabled clients and their families, as well as underpaid and unappreciated. She was beginning to feel used by her supervisior, her clients, and her lover.

INITIAL STAGE

Initially Ellen wanted to work on her feelings of burnout and on clarifying her interpersonal relationships. She was uneasy and noted that her last two attempts at therapy were brief and unhelpful. She wanted this time to work, but she was skeptical. She said she did not want to raise her expectations because she could not handle another disappointment.

As Ellen began slowly to explore family-of-origin dynamics which were replicated at work, such as an older critical supervisor who was much like her mother, she began to feel more optimistic. Her insight helped her begin to make some initial changes in her work environment and to look more closely at her relationship with her coworker. Unlike many professionals who want only to develop better coping stratagies, Ellen seemed motivated for real self-exploration. She began to realize that there were patterns in her life that continually reappeared. She longed to have a healthy and stable relationship with a man, as well as be able to feel satisfaction at work.

Her early disclosures involved instances when she attempted to serve or please others at her own expense. This seemed tied to her need for affection, approval, and acceptance, obviously contributing to burnout. After a number of weekly sessions, I proposed that therapy be twice a week; at this Ellen blushed. She seemed shocked, embarrassed that I thought she needed to come twice a week, an indication that she was worse than she thought. At the same time, she felt that my proposal meant she was accepted and that I liked her. She said she would think about it and see if she could afford it.

In the next session she talked about her tendency to give up control to others, resenting them and then leaving. She wanted to be more assertive in relationships. She noted how much she hates getting advice, especially from her older brother; she was beginning to recognize how this contributed to her burnout.

In talking about the affair with her colleague, she said she knew it wasn't healthy, but she was looking for some excitement. "I know it wasn't right, I would end up giving in, going against my intent to end it." When asked what she saw in him and what was in it for her, she said, "This guy always flirted. He made me feel special." Also, the fact that he was very smart appealed to her. This was a big problem for her. It was significant that she envied and admired her older brother, who is very intelligent.

From session #3:

THERAPIST: You realized from the beginning there was a problem, but there was some overriding factor.

ELLEN: I was attracted to something that was wrong. I was bored, unhappy at work and personally. He was an enigma. There was a mystique about him.

THERAPIST: Go on; say more.

ELLEN: It was his poker face. He hides his feelings and tries to act like nothing phases him. He's so unaffected, so neutral. It's hard for me to take, so I want him all the more.

A *few sessions later:*

THERAPIST: What keeps coming up is your yearning to be desired and feel special. That yearning carries a lot of power and causes you to do things that later you regret.

ELLEN: (*Talking about being on vacation with a woman friend*) Yeah, like the time I was on vacation, if a guy acts nice to us, or like we're special, then they have us. It could be almost anybody!

THERAPIST: Tell me more.

ELLEN: It finally came out a few years ago. I always thought my brother Owen (*six years older*) was mean to me because he just didn't like me. He was always criticizing me and yelling at me. But the truth was he resented that I was born because Alan would play with me. Alan was four when I was born. When Owen was at school, Alan and I always got along well.

THERAPIST: Like your older brother, Owen, lost his brother, Alan, to you.

ELLEN: I guess. He was so mean to me, even when he was in college. I would end up crying! Then came the turning point, when I was 18. My parents found out I wasn't a virgin. What a catastrophe! Then all of a sudden my brothers were very nice to me. (*She laughed.*) They said, "Hey, she's not so bad after all."

THERAPIST: So that was the way of gaining acceptance. That was the thing that made it with your brothers. Like somehow you had to use sex in order to be liked. The true test is to be desired in that kind of way. You referred to it as the turning point.

ELLEN: It was with them and with my parents. It was a very hard time. I had been the most well-behaved of all the kids. My mother freaked out and called in sick the next day. She couldn't even look at me without tears. She had to force herself to hug me. My father was upset but didn't show it very much. He lectured me on living up to their standards while living in their house and being an influence on my sister. But she knew things about me and our brothers they didn't know. Maria was more sexually active than me.

THERAPIST: Maybe what's happening now is somehow related to what happened then?

ELLEN: Yeah. I'm reminded of a conversation I had with a past supervisor about how it wouldn't be a good idea for us to get involved. He said he knew that if he really wanted me he could have me. It wasn't true! But that's how he dealt with the fact that we didn't have sex. It was in the air, on the agenda. But he did say I had a tendency to be accommodating and that I should not do things just to be nice, or because I was bored. How true! It's how I was brought up: to be nice to people and not to think about yourself. It's to a weird extreme with me, even sexually. It's important to me that he be sexually pleased (*referring to the coworker*), even more important to me than if I was "screwy" (*meaning going out of her mind*)

Ellen came in the next session feeling worn-out, tired, and without focus. She spoke of not wanting to go to work because of the situation with her married coworker.

ELLEN: I'm not a very happy person; no matter where I am. I'm not comfortable with myself. My tendency has always been to escape my situation; the problem is really me. I'm totally burned out.

She went on to talk about a romantic relationship she had in college. She heard from her college roommate that this former lover was getting married this summer. She said their relationship was on again, off again. She believes now that she got involved to confirm her desirability. Each time they got back together it was intense and exciting. When they were together over an extended period, it was harder to sustain the interest.

ELLEN: We had been always desperate to see each other, but then it started to deteriorate. When we got back together again it was great initially, then it wore off. He developed some doubts, then I pulled back.

She admitted that when they were apart she could not give up the fantasy that it might work out someday.

ELLEN: The relationship was mostly on his terms.
THERAPIST: Similar to now. (*The pattern was becoming increasingly apparent.*)
ELLEN: Yeah. As a matter of fact . . . I cancel something; he doesn't show. I would later tell him how I felt. He went on as if I never said anything. I finally told him I wanted to end the affair.
THERAPIST: I sense you haven't given him up emotionally—still dreaming he will choose you over his wife.
ELLEN: Yes—I even called him back the other day to see if it was still off. At least I don't have to wait for this guy's wedding announcement. (*She laughed, acknowledging that this man was already married.*)
THERAPIST: Since we're just about out of time today, we have to reschedule next Monday's meeting because I'll be out of town. Would you like to meet Friday of this week at 9 a.m.?
ELLEN: (*blushing*) I guess so.
THERAPIST: Why do you say, "I guess so"?
ELLEN: Because I do want to.
THERAPIST: Any idea? Are you afraid to say?
ELLEN: I'm embarrassed. I think I would like to come in twice a week.
THERAPIST: I don't understand why you're blushing?
ELLEN: I don't either.
THERAPIST: Embarrassed because I want to see you more?
ELLEN: I don't know. I guess because . . . (*long pause*).
THERAPIST: Because of sexual feelings?

ELLEN: I don't think so. (*Then, after a long but thoughtful pause*) Because I would like to come twice a week!

THERAPIST: I still don't understand.

ELLEN: Well, you didn't bring up the idea of coming twice a week again—you just said, "Would you like to meet that time?" Also I think it's two things. One, I'm embarrassed that I want to and need to, and two, I'm not real secure with you yet. I'd like to feel that you are genuinely concerned and have my best interest at heart.

THERAPIST: As opposed to?

ELLEN: As opposed to me just being a patient and you making money. And, so when you first said, "Do you want to come twice a week?" it's a trust thing going here.

THERAPIST: Once a week is a commitment. Twice a week even more a commitment.

ELLEN: Yes. But I need to solve my problem or else I'm not going to be any happier.

THERAPIST: But you're not sure that what I'm offering is what you need. Can you say more about that?

ELLEN: You've been very business-like and it's your business.

THERAPIST: You're not entirely happy about that, then?

ELLEN: Well, I don't know yet.

THERAPIST: You would wish that it be what?

ELLEN: I don't know, well, to say so many personal things, I'd like to know if they're being taken in and thought about by a person and that it's not just an unloading on my part, and that there would be continuity in your mind from one visit to the next.

THERAPIST: So you're not sure if that's true.

ELLEN: That's right!

THERAPIST: I can understand that there is a certain amount of frustration because it's hard for me to be of help until I get a better understanding of you. I'd rather not comment prematurely.

ELLEN: In (*the city where she lived previously*) I had a prepaid plan where I could have only a certain number of appointments. I went and he was falling asleep. I even forgot to tell you about this in our first session.

THERAPIST: Maybe there's a parallel because I've recently made some schedule changes and I'm asking you to come when I'm available, and so it's like, "Here we go again." But I'm committed to maintaining continuity as much as possible. I'm not going to be yanking you around like you've known all too well.

ELLEN: It is true, it's exactly the same situation. When I get to talking about something important (*with coworker*), then he has to go. Or when it gets uncomfortable for him, then he has to go. He says he has a meeting. How do I know what he really has to do? He always just leaves. And here, is the time up? Or do I have to keep track of the time?

THERAPIST: It is true we have to be careful about the time; for example, we have gone over today. But I think that reflects the fact that we haven't had enough time.

We then arranged a twice-a-week schedule.

ELLEN: The session is over now, right?

A few sessions later Ellen brought up her ambivalence about accepting money from her parents to fly home for a holiday weekend.

ELLEN: I shouldn't let them do that.

THERAPIST: Why not?

ELLEN: Because it makes me feel like I'm still dependent on them. It's kind of a gift, but there's no real need or reason for this, actually.

THERAPIST: You see a distinction between a gift and their need to support you? But you're not sure which this is?

ELLEN: They're saying it's a gift, but I would be accepting it as a need.

THERAPIST: Whose?

ELLEN: Mine.

THERAPIST: So what's wrong with that?

ELLEN: I always see my visits as something for me; not so much for them. I'm sure they don't see it that way.

THERAPIST: You seem to have a problem with having needs for you.

ELLEN: Like taking the time to come here.

THERAPIST: It reminds me of your feeling embarrassed about my suggestion to come twice a week.

Ellen spoke further about how hard it was to ask for the time off from work for the appointments as well as the extra time to make her flight home.

THERAPIST: So you're getting better at being okay about asking for something for you. It's been tough for you to admit that you need or even just want something.

ELLEN: I am selfish in some ways, like when I want to be by myself. But it is hard to ask or expect things from other people. It's better to give than to receive. "You should think of others first" was drummed into me. Mom said (*about the plane tickets*), "Don't feel bad, just be happy and say thank you." Gee, now they're telling me that I should take what they offer and be grateful. You know, when you get a gift, you're supposed to graciously say thank you, even if you don't like it. They always expected me to be grateful if they ever did anything for me even if they were completely out of touch with what I wanted. Maybe I'm afraid to ask for what I need not only because I might not get it, but also because if I do get it, then I'll have to pay somehow.

THERAPIST: But it's not only your receiving but also their giving. If this value is going to work there has to be people on the receiving end. Otherwise, giving would have no meaning. So if you make it hard for them to give, their value about giving can't be lived out, which you share to a certain extreme; so that makes it very hard for you to be a receiver.

ELLEN: I've been a difficult receiver this past year. Getting gifts, everything. I feel so obligated. Do I deserve this? Do I owe something now? Am I working hard enough?

The initial period of treatment was filled with memories of her brothers. She had observed and heard much about her brothers' sexual escapades. Many times after getting home from school she would see one of the girlfriend's cars parked in front of the house, her shoes inside the door and the door to her brother's bedroom closed. Once she accidently discovered Alan and his girlfriend making out in the woods behind their house. She had uneasy memories of sexual advances made by Owen. Once he came into her bedroom to kiss her goodnight, only the kiss was longer than usual and on the lips. She felt very uncomfortable about it and has a "creepy" feeling about it to this day. She said she never told anyone about this until now. She got more in touch with her anger at Owen because of his influence and control over her. She recalled many instances when she was teased and humiliated by him. Also she was supposed to keep her brothers' secrets from her parents. "My role was to be the most responsible."

THERAPIST: So you couldn't have those kinds of feelings or indulge in those kinds of activities. If you were aware of these things, in spite of your parents' teachings, you would think, "Why can't I do these things? It doesn't seem fair."

ELLEN: It made me question, What is right? If they could do it, I could, too. But should I?

THERAPIST: What about the time when you became sexually active?

ELLEN: I knew they felt it was wrong. When I was 16 I went with a boy for over a year. I was very curious about sex. Then all of a sudden he started to pressure me for sex. I was scared and confused. I didn't want to get pregnant. I really didn't want to be doing it. Finally, I consented; I gave in. And I knew I didn't want to. It was really stupid. I even

> knew he was dating another girl. After that, there was another guy. I knew by then that Mom assumed we were sexually active or worried I was. Later I did it because I assumed she thought I was. It's hard to talk about this. There was always this power and control thing, then the giving in and not wanting to. That happens too many times. I have to figure out how I feel about myself sexually.

Many of the early sessions were filled with painful memories alternating with stories of frustration and conflict at work. Like a lot of women, Ellen grew up with a complicated ambivalence about sex. On the one hand, she learned that it was selfish—and she'd eventually have to pay—to want things for herself. The boys who put so much pressure on her made her feel that sex was for them. If she didn't comply they wouldn't be interested in her. On the other hand, sex was exciting, part of the privileged world of her brothers. Her parents disapproved, but left them all unsupervised in the afternoon. Surely they knew what was going on. Despite what they said, did they somehow accept it? Expect it?

All this made her feel that there was something duplicitous, something not to be trusted, about her parents. She was never really sure that they meant what they said. And what about the therapist? She may expect or anticipate that his messages will be false, insincere, or not to be trusted or believed. In a subsequent session she said: "How can I believe you when I can't even believe my own parents?"

More and more reluctance emerged. In session #20, I wondered out loud if she was feeling vulnerable. She added, "resentful." She confessed behaving with me like with family: polite, unlike in the rest of her life. She was angry with herself for wasting time. She wanted to be open but found that when she arrived at the office she closed up.

Session #26: She slipped and used profanity in the hour for the first time, a sign of increasing comfort and some response to transference interpretations around being a father or elder brother figure. She also reported feeling new enthusiasm at work. Also, she began to note a greater caution in the way she approached new relationships; she has been slower to get involved.

Session #30: Ellen reported a dream where she was in my office getting undressed for a physical—denying any sexual aspect—reflecting, she thought, the fact that she was becoming more revealing in the therapy.

Session #31: She affirmed that therapy was helping her know more about what she needs. She gave examples of asserting herself with her boss, feeling confident in herself as a competent professional. She has been investing more at work with some beneficial results.

The early phase of therapy had enabled her to begin to clarify a pattern of lack of self-definition. In addition, a theme of wanting to be special was also emerging.

MIDDLE PHASE: GRANDIOSITY DEFENDED

Session #57: Ellen spoke about not acknowledging her ambitions: wanting children and a successful private practice someday. She also became aware of defending against the overstimulation of being in a good place: like being in psychotherapy. She said, "I can barely stand it!"

We reviewed her negative feeling about prior therapists and many prior relationships (mostly boyfriends). If she lets herself get established in a good place, she has to risk rejection, empathic failure, and even feeling indulged and gratified in reality. She expressed fears about whether the results and benefits, as well as the therapy itself, would last.

Sessions #58–61: She questioned her need to be in therapy because she is "successful" by society's standards. Again, it is hard for her to accept something that is just for her. She questioned whether the therapy is "medically necessary," which is the basis of her eligibility for insurance coverage. This reminded me of how she felt when I suggested she come twice a week, as well as the time her parents bought her plane tickets.

After interpreting her reservation to "show herself" based on her upbringing that it was bad to be immodest, she recalled times at age 11 or 12 of embarrassment over getting an award and being chosen to be on TV. Instead of getting praised by her family, she got teased.

She didn't want to be on display. She perceived my efforts to get her to talk as manipulative. She saw me as forcing her to produce (like her brother Owen, who was the smartest of the kids and always emphasized the importance of getting good grades). She didn't want to give certain things up right then, and came only because she "should." She viewed therapy as an infringement on her privacy.

She insisted that she doesn't want to do what other people want if she doesn't want to. She then admitted that, nevertheless, if I say anything in a session she has to take it seriously.

Over the next 20–30 sessions there was a shift into exploration of rivalrous feelings with her mother and sister. Themes predominate about "the other woman" or her being "the other woman." She recalled feelings of being displaced by her sister when she was two as the one and only daughter. This was exacerbated by Maria's prematurity and heightened parental concern for several months following Maria's arrival. Ellen actively pitched in as Mommy's little helper and to this day remains deferential to her "sisters." Insights around these issues enabled her to better understand her mixed feelings toward the newly hired counselor at her agency. She immediately started to go out of her way to be helpful to the new member of the team, all the while sensing an uneasy resentment and a feeling that she was being ignored by her director.

Session #92: She decided to end the relationship with her boyfriend. "I'd rather be alone with myself than miserable with a bad relationship."

Session #95: She expressed her discomfort and shame about running for an office in her local professional organization. She feared that her ideas would not be appreciated enough to be followed. More came out about the shame associated with getting praised; more about her difficulty being a receiver. After she spoke about her fears of being embraced by another woman (she freezes), the fear of her dependent needs was interpreted. She was eventually able to admit that she wanted to be famous but was still embarrassed by attention and recognition.

Session #99: She was reminded again of her tendency to freeze up when close, especially with her father. They rarely had intimate conversations and barely knew what to talk about other than their work. She also tended to freeze up in the transference. I acknowledged how important it was for her to voice her feelings toward me. She wanted closeness but blocked this in various ways. At times she would fall silent, other times become irritable and angry.

Session #100: Ellen disclosed more feelings of powerlessness, fearing failure, reactivation of self-doubts and assumptions about being weak. She wants to move ahead, but feels she has to cling to what closeness she has, that is, to resume the relationship with boyfriend. Then she reiterated examples of relationships that were inadequate and faulty.

Session #101: She related an incident at work where she felt unsupported and was left feeling tired, depleted, and angry. But gradually she was coming to a sense of gaining acceptance, if not comfort, with weakness and limits. She speaks more affirmatively about leaving exploiters, as well as her own impulses to retaliate, behind.

Session #105: She reported feeling better but not trusting this feeling. She never learned to be comfortable with the idea of feeling good, just for herself. If she was busy doing things for other people, then she felt safe. But just being happy, was that really okay?

Session #107: She made another visit home. It was more positive this time. She felt much less reactive, much less anxious. Ellen was able to talk openly with her sister and each parent. She came to feel more accepting of not living near her family. Her level of differentiation of self and her ability to be nonreactive were improving.

My notes at about 18 months provided this summary:

> Ellen, almost 30, with depressive and narcissistic features as well as problematic interpersonal relationships, presented a year and a half ago with symptoms of burnout. She was exhausted, unhappy, irritable, and confused. She had lost confidence and any sense of satisfaction or pleasure from her work. She has strengthened her sense of self and ability to regulate her mood. She has gradually developed greater clarification about wants and needs, both occupationally and personally. She has become more appropriately assertive and is better able to say, no. Over the past six months, oedipal themes have emerged and predominate; analysis of sibling relationships has given way to focus on parental relationships and their contemporary manifestations at work and in her social life. She is aware of the need for more practice (working-through) of her newfound insights, and is still moderately insecure about the solidity of her new cohesion. Although group therapy might be a reasonable approach now, it will be important to address the transference that has developed and its continuing analysis.

Sessions #120 and 121: She reports many activities in her life, feelings of invigoration as well as fears of losing her new sense of personal power and well-being. Ellen now has multiple male and female friends. She senses that men have an unspoken romantic interest in her. She no longer seems to seek this flattery, although she at times still gets some mileage out of it. She is more aware of the problem of being idolized, now that she feels more self-accepting.

Session #150: Ellen got a major boost in her self-esteem from getting supervisory responsibility for a graduate student assigned to her agency. She expressed some worry that if I saw her work I would judge her negatively. While easily intimidated by people whom she views as good and successful, she is able to bask in her elevated status.

She seems to do best when I'm able to stay out of her way. If she is ever interrupted or cut off she is reminded of her mother, who was well-known for doing this. A painful example of this was when Ellen called home from college to discuss transferring and coming back home to live. At some point early in this conversation her mother broke in to tell her about their plans to rent out her room to a local college student.

Session #156: Ellen registered her awareness of keeping her social life separate from "family (work) life." It dawned on her that relations with men have been "incestuous," in that they have often been with coworkers, employees, etc.

Session #170: Therapy seemed bogged down. After gentle inquiry, Ellen spoke of my meaning more to her than she to me (where she is one of many patients, "women"). She expressed the desire to have the ignored part of herself recognized. She was disappointed that I had not responded more excitedly to her becoming a supervisor. She had concluded that her talent and skill for this was "no good," a cause for embarrassment. But she has been getting positive feedback from her student as well as from the program director.

Here is a good example of a disruption in psychotherapy that is an inevitable, necessary component of the disruption-restoration process and eventually brings about healing. This hurting, uncertain woman learned to hide herself away. Now, in therapy, she's gradually opening up—being more honestly and fully herself, making herself vulnerable in the process. What I said (or failed to say) or did hurt her and she reacted by shutting down—a form of silent rage. When this sequence of events is identified and acknowledged things can be different. She let me know she was hurt, and I didn't argue or defend myself. I acknowledged her feelings and I acknowledged her. Each disruption (of the selfobject bond) provided an occasion for reexperiencing old injuries still in need of healing. Often, when patients feel understood in their efforts at self-preservation and defensive maneuvers, they may be able for the first time to consider giving them up.

Session #186: She is beginning to express intense negative feelings toward me: (1) When I joke, she feels I laugh at her. In her family, all the joking was at the expense of others. "My family was cruel." She wanted me to know it is very risky to make jokes in her therapy. (2) When she talked about getting obscene phone calls recently she felt upset when I "judged" that others would not have stayed on the phone to be harassed. She told me it was like I was blaming the rape victim for "asking for it."

I tried to positively accept her feeling expressions. It was hard at first, but I knew she was right. I let her know that I understood and accepted what she was saying. She was greatly relieved. Not only did she have the opportunity to lower her defenses (her offensive) but she was also able to experience greater self-acceptance. As I was able to empathize with her (and myself), she was able to internalize this function and expand her own capacity for empathy for self and others.

Session #191: Her approach-avoidance with men played out with me. She clung to my every word, even yawn; she reacted with humiliation, disgust, insult and rage when I failed to hear her or adequately understand her. Psychotherapy fostered her opening herself to her needs and feelings, which temporarily made her more dependent and vulnerable. While she hoped for a new beginning, she also dreaded that her history of being slighted would repeat itself, that she would be traumatized again.

Session #192: She was trying to stay conscious of keeping separate boundaries at work and balancing what she needed to do with her desire to help and work with people. She was beginning to realize how important boundaries are.

She said she had been too casual and informal with many of her patients and their families, "just trying to be friendly." She was spending too much time out of the hospital running errands for families that were unnecessary and not really part of her responsibility. "I guess I wanted them to like me." It was always a problem finding the time to complete the basic tasks that were expected. She often found herself working late into the evening.

She noted she was becoming a better listener. "Remember that day I blasted you?" (session #186) You didn't try to defend yourself. You just listened. That helped me a lot! I realized that if my patients are upset or dissatisfied it doesn't necessarily mean that I have to do something. Also I realized that your faults and limitations were not going to be disastrous to my therapy. I actually thought I was giving you some pretty sound advice. She laughed.

She recalled a family vacation when she got lost in a parking lot and was frantically searching for her family. She was panic-stricken. When she eventually found her parents they had not missed her. To this day they are unaware of the height of her anxiety that day. She concluded they "always assumed I could take care of myself," and realized how often they were unaware of what she needed.

In this context, I very tentatively brought up the idea of having her family visit her and all of them coming in with her for a family conference. At this she was terrified. She realized she was still protecting them.

She was the good girl growing up and her siblings were rebels. Now they are highly successful, and she feels that she is a disappointment in the eyes of her father. She paid an early price by self-sacrificing her own goals, ideals, and ambitious in order to gain a sense of belonging that she never achieved. Now she is trying to find her way with great pain and with reluctance to ask for help and support.

Session #212: She is becoming more productive at work and receiving glowing evaluations. She is not sure what to make of all these positive statements.

She was able to see more clearly what she was bringing to the therapy relationship that was separate from what I contributed in the way of adversity and misunderstanding.

Session #212: She talked about seeing her father as depressed all his life, perceiving him as a pathetic hoax. At first this caught me by surprise, but I came to see her reaction as part of her discovering her rage, i.e., a transitional step from self-doubt and loathing to self-respect. He was not there for her, which led to self-doubt. If he had no interest (response) in her, "something must be wrong with me" (after all, he is a psychologist).

Then, she developed her sense of obligation and responsibility for the welfare—even survival—of others. She could feel a split within herself: the dutiful, sacrificial daughter vs. the talented, carefree, creative person.

Ellen paid a heavy price in her development in order to win favor and acceptance—she was always so polite. She brought up the fact that she had been having some suicidal thoughts. Her self-hatred now is related to her failure to be herself. I suggested that she failed to recognize the amount of real pressure she was subject to that molded her this way. I recommended she not take total blame for the outcome. She expressed an awareness of loving herself more than her family, as well as hating herself more.

She recalled a family photo with her standing off to the side. I tried to interpret her distancing herself as a healthy move toward self-preservation.

Session #230: Ellen dreamt again of being pregnant. She was looking cheerful and animated. Looking pensive, she said, "Can strength result from feeling so weak?"

Session #240: Things seemed to be coming together: feeling job satisfaction, telling a prospective date no, making more social efforts with women, feeling more joyful about herself and seeing value in her selfness.

At work Ellen noticed she was enthusiastic again. As a result of therapy she was perceiving and acting differently. She was more sensitive to the needs and feelings of others. Moreover, she felt her colleagues were attentive and friendlier toward her. Since she felt more secure and that she really did belong, this made her happier and more productive. Even though she had one of the largest caseloads, she didn't really mind, because she was enjoying her work and getting home at a decent hour.

Ironically, it seemed that with expanded responsibility as a supervisor she felt less burdened by her job and more highly valued and esteemed.

Session #244: She reported the most significant family visit since therapy started. This followed the proposal that they come see her for a family visit. Much was said from both sides. Her mother spoke of a special bond she felt with Ellen that she had never voiced because of guilt feelings. Ellen expressed her observations of her mother's significant capacity for imprecise empathy, leading to repeated failures of attention and responsivity. She expressed her concerns about father's possible depression. She also told them of her recent thoughts and fears of suicide. She described moving moments of tears. She and I both had a sense of her great achievement. She conveyed a sense of it being a mutual accomplishment of hers and mine. She said that she feels she has forgiven her parents and herself.

Session #250: She is doing well in all areas! She was starting to develop a new relationship with a man.

FINAL PHASE

After almost three and a half years

Session #256: It seems Ellen has entered termination phase of therapy.

Session #271: There is some struggle with give-and-take in new relationship. She is afraid of causing alienation and eventual abandonment. The boyfriend seems to be afraid of intimacy. Is this because she needs too much? She is wary because she doesn't want to make another major mistake.

Session #280: There is evidence of new self-structure and resolution of intrapsychic conflicts. She is much better able to surmount slights and rage reactions. She feels much less susceptible to being under the undue influence of another.

Session #282: Ellen reports they have discussed marriage and moving in together (after four months of dating).

Session #293: Ellen seems to be handling the ups and downs well. A termination date is set about three months off.

Session #294: Some reactive (termination) depression is setting in.

Session #304: Evidence shows of increasing comfort with her decision to end the therapy as well as moving in with her boyfriend.

Session #307: At a country fair she found the perfect metaphor for herself: Her boyfriend's six-year-old niece wanted to have her face painted by a clown but she was afraid to ask. She always wanted to say, "Look at me!" and be responded to with an embracing acceptance.

Session #309: She's grieving giving up the single life, but not yet ready to marry. Again, she doesn't want to make a mistake. She says she learned in therapy to have her feelings—even though she is still frightened at times.

Session #312: She talked about some of her new attitudes toward her work. She believes she went into social work because she wanted to help people who had "something wrong with them." More recently, because of therapy, she has been in touch with her long buried conviction about being weak and flawed. She can now say how this is true and false. It is not as true as she once thought (as a small child), but also not entirely without grounding in her mortality and limitation as a human being. In fact, she feels she has become more patient and empathic with her patients because of her deeper and broader perspective on the tragic in life.

Ellen seemed to have a sense of the wounded healer idea (experience) without having actually employed the phrase. She knew now, at a deep level, that she had to look after her own wounds and at the same time be prepared to heal the wounds of others. She was learning how to make her wounds into a major source of her healing power. She was discovering how strength can result from facing her vulnerability and shame.

> . . . the wound of loneliness is like the Grand Canyon—a deep incision in the surface of our existence which has become an inexhaustible source of beauty and self-understanding. . . . When we become aware that we do not have to escape our pains, but that we can mobilize them into a common search for life, those very pains are transformed from expressions of despair into signs of hope. (Nouwen, 1972, pp. 84, 93)

Session #316: This was our final session. She exhibited a full range of affect in her comprehensive summary and review of her psychotherapy. She spoke of the positive results of the therapy in her life—in her friendships, her family, and her work. There were tears of sadness and expression of satisfaction and the sense of a great accomplishment.

She also told me something she had not before revealed:

how mortified she felt when wetting her pants in the second grade. This seemed an apt way to end the therapy. I sensed multiple levels of meaning in this, her final communication to me:

1. This was her way of telling me she had no more secrets; there was no more holding back.
2. She had come full circle from her initial complaint at the start of therapy that her life was out of control. Here she was saying that I never really knew the complete story of the depth of her sense of failure and incompetence, which reached to the level of her basic physiological functioning.
3. I was able to create an atmosphere that helped her deepen the pain to a level where it could be shared. She could now expect that her pain would be understood and felt, that she no longer had to run away from it but could accept it as an expression of her basic human condition.
4. Her confession announced the deepening of hope that sharing weakness is a reminder of the coming strength.

Treatment lasted a little over four years. The major problem, in contrast to her distressing symptoms, came under the rubric of mood and self-esteem regulation. She had many of the hallmarks of burnout at the start, and this work depletion was a recurring feature during three of the four years. She often wondered what had become of her idealism and dedication. Though she was always able to keep herself going, she was easily fatigued.

After about three years of twice-a-week psychotherapy, she developed a significant but transient depression, with some suicidal features. Extra sessions and frequent phone calls were employed to support her through this phase. The depression seemed to result from a deepening of the therapy process and much working-through followed. The remainder of the treatment went rapidly and well. The first two-three years were characterized by much hesitancy, guardedness, and shame.

With increasing structuralization via interpretations in the context of a mirroring selfobject transference, she became a vigorous, vital, and animated person in a sustained way. During the final year of therapy she was in her most successful romantic relationship. At times there was heated conflict but Ellen and her boyfriend both seemed to have a strong commitment to work out and talk about their misunderstandings and differences. Nevertheless, I had the sense that her relationship with the boyfriend was not necessary for the mainteinance of her well-being. Even if the relationship failed, she would have the resilience and strength to weather the loss and proceed from a solid independent center of initiative and healthy self-assertion.

BIBLIOGRAPHY

Allen, D. (1979). Hidden stresses in success. *Psychiatry*, 42, 171–175.

Barnhill, L., & Longo, D. (1979). Fixation and regression in the family life cycle. *Family Process*, 17(4).

Baruch, D. (1952). *One little boy*. New York: Dell.

Bateson, G. (1972). *Steps to an ecology of mind*. New York: Ballantine.

Beavers, W. R. (1977). *Psychotherapy and growth*. New York: Brunner/Mazel.

Beavers, W. R., & Hampson, R. B. (1990). *Successful families: Assessment and intervention*. New York: W. W. Norton.

Beavers, W. R., Lewis, J. M., Gossett, J. T., & Phillips, V. A. (1975, May). Family systems and ego functions: Midrange families. *Scientific Proceedings* (Summary #265). Presented at the 128th Meeting of the American Psychiatric Association, Anaheim, CA.

Berkowitz, M. (1987). Therapist survival: maximizing generativity and minimizing burnout. *Psychotherapy in Private Practice*, 5(1), 85–89.

Bierce, A. (1911). *The devil's dictionary*. New York: Dover.

Bion, W. R. (1961). *Experience in groups*. London: Tavistock Publications.

Bion, W. R. (1967). *Notes on memory and desire. Psychoanalytic Forum*, 2, 271–280.

Black, C. (1982). *It will never happen to me*. Colorado: M.A.C. Publications.

Boisen, A. T. (1954). *Out of the depths—an autobiographical study of mental disorder and religious experience*. New York: Harper and Brothers.

Bowen, M. (1978). *Family therapy in clinical practice.* New York: Jason Aronson.
Brown, F. H. (1991). *Reweaving the family tapestry.* New York: W. W. Norton.
Bugental, J. (1990). *Intimate journeys.* San Francisco: Jossey-Bass.
Carter, E. A., & McGoldrick, M. (1980). *The family life cycle.* New York: Gardner Press.
Carter, E. A., & McGoldrick, M. (1989). *The changing family life cycle* (2nd ed.). Boston: Allyn & Bacon.
Chodorow, N. (1978). *The reproduction of mothering: Psychoanalysis and the sociology of gender.* Berkeley: University of California Press.
Clark, G., & Vaccaro, J. (1987). Burnout among CMHC psychiatrists and the struggle to survive. *Hospital and Community Psychiatry, 38*(8), 843–847.
Cooper, A. (1986). Some limitations on therapeutic effectiveness: The "burnout syndrome" in psychoanalysis. *Psychoanalytic Quarterly, 55*(4), 576–598.
Daniel, S., & Rogers, M. (1981, Fall). Burnout and the pastorate: A critical review with implication for pastors. *Journal of Psychology and Theology, 9*(3), 232–249.
Farber, B. (1983). *Stress and burnout in the human service professions.* New York: Pergamon Press.
Fassell, D. (1990). *Working ourselves to death.* San Francisco: Harper San Francisco.
Freudenberger, H. (1974). Staff burnout. *Journal of Social Issues, 30*(1), 159–165.
Freudenberger, H. (1980). *Burnout: The high cost of high achievement.* New York: Doubleday.
Friedman, E. (1985). *Generation to generation.* New York: Guilford Press.
Friedman, R. (1985). Making family therapy easier for the therapist: Burnout preventions. *Family Process, 24*, 549–553.
Gilligan, C. (1982). *In a different voice.* Cambridge: Harvard University Press.
Groesbeck, C. J. (1975). The archetypal image of the wounded healer. *Journal of Analytical Psychology, 20*, 122–145.
Guggenbuhl-Craig, C. A. (1971). *Power in the helping professions.* New York: Springer Publications.
Guy, J. (1987). *The personal life of the psychotherapist.* New York: John Wiley & Sons.
Hart, A. (1991). *Adrenaline and stress.* Texas: Word Publishing.
Heitzenrater, R. P. (1984). *The elusive Mr. Wesley.* Nashville: Abingdon Press.
Hendrick, I. (1943). Work and the pleasure principle. *Psychoanalytic Quarterly, 2*, 311–329.
Himle, D., Jayaratne, S., & Chess, W. (1987). Gender differences in work stress among clinical social workers. *Journal of Social Service Research, 10*(1), 41–56.

Hopkins, G. M. (1948). Felix Randal. In: R. Bridges & W. H. Gardner (Eds.), *Poems of Gerard Manley Hopkins* (pp. 91–92). New York: Oxford University Press.

James, W. (1902). *The varieties of religious experience*. New York: Doubleday.

Jesse, R. (1989). *Children in recovery*. New York: W. W. Norton.

Jesse, R. (1990). *Healing the hurt*. Minneapolis: Johnson Institute.

Jones, E. (1951). The god complex. *Essays in applied psychoanalysis*. Vol. II. (pp. 244–265). London: Hogarth Press.

Jung, C. G. (1968). *Analytic psychology: Its theory and practice*. New York: Pantheon.

Jung, C. G. (1951). *Fundamental questions of psychotherapy. Collected works*. Princeton: Princeton University Press.

Kerenyi, C. (1959). *Asklepios: Archetypal image of the physician's existence* (R. Manheim, Trans.). New York: Pantheon Books.

Kerr, M., & Bowen, M. (1988). *Family evaluation*. New York: W. W. Norton.

Kestenbaum, J. (1984, June). Expectations for therapeutic growth: One factor in burnout. *Social Casework: The Journal of Contemporary Social Work*, 374–377.

Kligerman, C. (1989). The search for the self of the future analyst. In A. Goldberg (Ed.), *Dimensions of self experience: Progress in self psychology*, Vol. 5 (pp. 253–268). Hillsdale, NJ: Analytic Press.

Knight, J. A. (1986). The religio-psychological dimension of wounded healers. In L. H. Robinson (Ed.), *Psychiatry and religion: Overlapping concerns* (pp. 34–49). Washington, DC: American Psychiatric Press, Inc.

Kohut, H. (1984). *How does analysis cure?* Chicago: University of Chicago Press.

Kohut, H. (1978). *The search for the self*. New York: International Universities Press.

Kohut, H. (1971). *The analysis of the self*. New York: International Universities Press.

Kottler, J. (1986). *On being a therapist*. San Francisco: Jossey-Bass.

Lavandero, R. (1981, November–December). Nurse burnout: What can we learn? *The Journal of Nursing Administration*, 17–23.

Lee, R. R. (1988). The reverse selfobject experience. *American Journal of Psychotherapy*, 42(3), 416–424.

Lewis, J. M., Beavers, W. R., Gossett, J. R., & Phillips, V. A. (1976). *No single thread: Psychological health in family systems*. New York: Brunner/Mazel.

Lichtenberg, J. D. (1991). What is a self object? *Psychoanalytic Dialogues*, *1*(4), 455–479.

Liddle, H., Breunlin, D., & Schwartz, R. (Eds.). (1988). *Handbook of family therapy training and supervision*. New York: Guilford Press.

Maeder, T. (1989). *Children of psychiatrists and other psychotherapists*. New York: Harper and Row.

Marmor, J. (1953, November). The feeling of superiority: An occupational hazard in the practice of psychotherapy. *American Journal of Psychiatry*, 370–376.
McGoldrick, M., & Gerson, R. (1985). *Genograms in family assessment*. New York: W. W. Norton.
Meier, C. A. (1967). *Ancient incubation and modern psychotherapy* (M. Curtis, Trans.). Chicago: Northwestern University Press.
Miller, A. (1979). The drama of the gifted child and the psychoanalyst's narcissistic disturbance. *International Journal of Psychoanalysis, 60*, 47–58.
Miller, J. B. (1976). *Toward a new psychology of women*. Boston: Beacon Press.
Moore, T. (1992). *Care of the soul*. New York: HarperCollins.
Morrison, A. P. (1989). *Shame: The underside of narcissism*. Hillsdale, NJ: Analytic Press.
Nichols, M. (1987). *The self in the system: Expanding the limits of family therapy*. New York: Brunner/Mazel.
Notman, M., & Nadelson, C. (1991). *Women and men: New perspectives on gender differences*. Washington, DC: American Psychiatric Press, Inc.
Nouwen, H. J. (1972). *The wounded healer*. Garden City, NY: Doubleday.
Olsen, D., & Grosch, W. (1991). Clergy burnout: A self psychology and systems perspective. *Journal of Pastoral Care, 45*, 297–304.
Peterson, M. R. (1992). *At personal risk*. New York: W. W. Norton.
Pines, A. (1993). *Burnout: Handbook of stress* (pp. 386–402). New York: Free Press.
Pines, A., & Aronson, E. (1988). *Career burnout: Causes and cures* (2nd ed.). New York: Free Press.
Raider, M. (1989). Burnout in children's agencies: A clinician's perspective. *Residential Treatment for Children and Youth*, 6(3), 43–51.
Raquepaw, J., & Miller, R. (1989). Psychotherapist burnout: a componential analysis. *Professional Psychotherapy: Research and Practice*, 20(1), 32–36.
Rogers, E. (1987). Professional burnout: A review of a concept. *The Clinical Supervisor*, 5(3), 91–106.
Rosenblatt, A., & Mayer, J. (1975). Objectional supervisory styles: Student's views. *Social Work*, 20(3), 184–189.
Schofield, W. (1964). *Psychotherapy: The purchase of friendship*. Englewood, NJ: Prentice-Hall.
Stevenson, R. (1989). Professional burnout in medicine and the helping professions. *Loss, Grief and Care*, 3(1–2), 33–38.
Stolorow, R., & Lachman, F. (1980). *Psychoanalysis of developmental arrests*. New York: International Universities Press.
Stoltenberg, C., & Delworth, R. (1987). *Supervising counselors and therapists: A developmental approach*. San Francisco: Jossey-Bass.
Suran, B., & Sheridan, E. (1985). Management of burnout: Training psy-

chologists in professional life span perspectives. *Professional Psychology: Research and Practice, 16*(6), 741–752.

Szasz, T. (1956). On the experiences of the analyst in the psychoanalytic situation. *Journal of the American Psychoanalytic Association, 4,* 197–223.

Tillich, P. (1952). *The courage to be.* New Haven: Yale University Press.

von Bertalanffy, L. (1968). *General systems theory.* New York: George Braziller.

Weinberg, R., & Mauksch, L. (1991). Examining family-of-origin influences in life at work. *Journal of Marriage and Family Therapy, 17*(3), 233–242.

Welt, S., & Herron, W. (1990). *Narcissism and the psychotherapist.* New York: Guilford Press.

Wing, J. C. (1977). *The limits of standardization in psychiatric diagnosis.* New York: Brunner/Mazel.

Wittgenstein, L. (1973). *Philosophical investigations.* New York: Macmillan.

Woititz, J. (1983). *Adult children of alcoholics.* Deerfield Beach, FL: Health Communications.

Wolf, E. (1989). *Treating the self.* New York: Guilford Press.

World Health Organization. (1992). *International classification of diseases* (10th ed.). (ICD-10), Geneva: WHO.

Yalom, I. (1985). *The theory and practice of group psychotherapy* (3rd ed.). New York: Basic Books.

INDEX